the Simplicity *of* HEALING

a PRACTICAL GUIDE to
Releasing the Miracle Power of
GOD'S WORD

DR. SANDRA G. KENNEDY

 Unless otherwise identified, Scripture quotations are taken from the New King James Version. All emphasis within Scripture quotations is the author's own.

It's Supernatural and Messianic Vision Inc.
4301 Westinghouse Blvd.
Charlotte, NC 28273

Cover design by Eileen Rockwell

ISBN 13 TP: 978-0-7684-1519-3
ISBN 13 eBook: 978-0-7684-1520-9
ISBN 13 HC: 978-0-7684-1521-6
ISBN 13 LP: 978-0-7684-1522-3

For Worldwide Distribution, Printed in the U.S.A.
3 4 5 6 7 8 / 21 20 19 18 17

CONTENTS

Foreword *by Sid Roth* 5

Introduction 9

Chapter 1 I Needed a Miracle 11

Chapter 2 I Got My Miracle!. 21

Chapter 3 Healing: He's Made It Simple 29

Chapter 4 An Unshakeable Faith 43

Chapter 5 Believing God Is the Key to Life 53

Chapter 6 I Have Believed, Therefore I Speak 65

Chapter 7 The Power of Agreement. 75

Chapter 8 Rise Above! 89

Chapter 9 Keep Your Eyes on Jesus 101

Chapter 10 Be Courageous! .115

Chapter 11 Keep On Keeping On! 127

Chapter 12 Matters of the Heart 137

Summary of Healing Principles 147

Healing Scriptures 151

Are You Born Again? 155

FOREWORD

by Sid Roth

When I first interviewed Dr. Sandra Kennedy for my It's Supernatural! television show, I was impressed that her teaching on healing was not just theory, but actually worked in her own life. Her testimony of a miraculous healing after her dog bit off part of her lip was the best practical experiential teaching I had ever heard. Her faith is tenacious!

I have found that combining teaching with the Word of God and step-by-step examples, as Sandra does, not only builds your faith, but simplifies the teaching process.

This teaching is right on time—we are on the verge of a great evangelistic healing and miracle revival. The

Word and revelation of the Word will continue to play a major role, but the manifestation of healings and miracles will accelerate.

God is in a hurry to get people saved. Why? Because He is coming back soon. He told me this three times in a dream. God's plan "A" for evangelism is always to demonstrate the Kingdom through signs and wonders to earn the right to present the King.

In less than three years, over 5,000 Jewish people in Israel have made public professions of faith in my own ministry outreaches by using God's plan "A." These types of numbers have not been seen in Israel since the Book of Acts. What's the difference maker? Signs and wonders!

I believe that in this next move of God, signs and wonders will be demonstrated by a vast army of Christians who have been spectators up till now. God is calling your name. It's the last act of the last play before Jesus returns. Will you remain a spectator, or will you be like Abraham? When God called Abraham, he responded, "Here am I!"

If you are willing, Sandra can help you. As you absorb her rich teaching, you will find yourself becoming normal—normal as defined by the Bible!

Jesus described this imminent end-time move of God's Spirit in John 14:12: "*...the works that I do he will* *do also; and greater works than these he will do."* These "greater works" will be creative miracles. Get ready for arms and legs and eyes and other missing body parts to appear before your eyes! I know I intend to move in the fullest of this new outpouring of God's Spirit. What about you? Your name is being called. What do you say?

INTRODUCTION

I'm privileged to share with you the healing principles the Lord has taught me over many years, principles based on the Word of God. God's Word is powerful—powerful enough to cause disease and pain to leave your body and bring healing and wholeness, powerful enough to change your circumstances and transform your whole life. God's Word is foundational to a victorious walk and receiving from Him all the blessings of redemption. I've witnessed untold numbers of people receive their healing by believing and standing on God's Word.

I've built my life upon the solid rock of the Word. God and His Word have brought me through many a storm and given me the strength to stand and remain steady through it all. I have personally experienced the healing power of God's Word, and my prayer is that you too will come to a personal knowledge of its healing and delivering power. God's Word is the key that unlocks the door for you to step into freedom from disease and step into that abundant life that Jesus provided for us. By the power of God's Word you can conquer anything and everything the enemy sends your way and continue to conquer all the days of your life. You'll find out how in the pages of this book.

This book focuses primarily on the power of God's Word to bring physical healing; however, these principles apply to every area of our lives—health, emotions, family, finances, relationships, employment, security...every area. The Word of God is a priceless treasure that will impact every area of your life and enable you to be triumphant in every situation. Put your faith in God's Word. It will never fail you. It will transform your whole life!

Chapter 1

I NEEDED A MIRACLE

"Where is your lip?" That's the question the emergency room nurse asked me on the night of November 7, 2000. I had just had an accidental encounter with my little dog. She jumped up as I was bending forward to get up off the sofa, and her mouth caught my lip as she was coming down. The bleeding was profuse and I grabbed a towel and held it over my mouth but never did look at it. My answer to the nurse's question was, "I don't know." I had just arrived at the emergency room and did not realize that half of my upper lip was missing. I was told by the surgeon that it could not be fixed. He said I would never be able to smile again and my speech would be affected. That's a very disconcerting thing for anyone to hear, but especially for a preacher.

I had known since I was a child that I was going to be involved with healing. At the age of nine, I heard the Lord speak that to me. I was outside in my yard, and all of a sudden I heard the Lord say, "One day, I will use you in the healing ministry." Up to that point, I had never heard a message on healing or seen anyone healed. That wasn't something my church taught. But when I heard the Lord speak that, I said to myself, "OK," not knowing what it all meant. I would pray as a child for sickly animals to be healed, even for dead ones to be raised up! I must admit I never saw any positive results at that time, but one thing I did know was that I would be used in healing in some fashion.

Over the years, I have seen firsthand the healing power of God's Word. One of the first miracles I witnessed was with my own mother who was dying of cancer. My family called me home because Mama was in a coma and the doctors said she only had a few days to live. On the airplane the Lord spoke to me and said, "Tell your mother, 'Our Father which art in heaven, hallowed be thy name. Thy kingdom come, thy will be done *in earth as it is in heaven.*' Tell your mother *there is no sickness in heaven!*"

I wanted a confirmation that I was to do that so I said, "Lord, tell someone else!" When I arrived home late at night, I discovered He had spoken the very same thing to my sister in a dream. The next day she and I began speaking that one thing to Mama over and over: "Our Father which art in heaven, hallowed be thy name. Thy kingdom come, thy will be done in earth as it is in heaven. Mama, there is no sickness in heaven!" Despite the fact Mama was in a coma as we sat by her side, we continued to repeat those words for five hours. Finally, she opened her eyes but was barely conscious. While I was sitting by the bed, I asked my mother, "Do you want to live?" I told her, "We are standing at a crossroads." Having been a youth pastor for many years, I went back to an illustration I had used many times. We stand at a crossroads in life, and at some point we must choose—Heaven or hell. Ultimately it's our choice. It's the same with healing as it is with salvation. It's a choice. Healing versus death. I said to her, "Mama, you have said maybe it's God's will that you die. But what if it's *your* choice. Live or die. What would you choose?"

She replied, "Live, stupid!"

I knew right then and there Mama was getting better! I said, "OK. Then we agree. You will live!" And she grabbed hold of that precious concept.

At one point I felt the Lord was telling me to anoint her with oil. I knew that was in the Bible somewhere, but I had never done that before; in fact, I had never even seen anyone anointed with oil. But I knew that's what we were supposed to do. My sister and I dragged Mama, who was barely conscious, to the kitchen and sat her in a chair with us holding her up. We searched the kitchen and all we could find was a can of Crisco shortening. So we held her up in the chair and slathered her all over with Crisco! We didn't know how much oil to use or even where to put it. We figured if "a little dab will do ya" then more would be even better! We covered her all over! Like we say in the country, we greased her up like a hog! And we kept speaking what the Lord had given us to speak. After several more hours, she got up out of that chair and walked to the bathroom by herself. She had been suffering with constipation for a week, but no longer. She was totally healed from cancer! Doctors later confirmed the cancer was gone, and they actually wrote on the front of her medical chart, "MIRACLE." My mother lived another twenty-seven years after that. Since that time, I have experienced the healing power of God's Word many times in my own life, and I've seen His healing power work in countless others.

After I graduated from college I attended Southwestern Baptist Theological Seminary in Dallas,

Texas. In 1973, I was visited by the Lord in an open vision. In the vision He showed me the future site of our ministry and spoke many things to me about how we would conduct the ministry. I had the exact same vision and heard the exact same words from the Lord again in 1980 and again in 1983. In the meantime, I saw many healing miracles as I would pray for folks.

It took me eleven years to process all of this and get past religion and tradition to do what God said I was to do. I had asked the opinions of many men, and they all told me I couldn't do it. After the second visitation, I began to share the vision, and I also received the baptism of the Holy Spirit. I determined to do what God told me to do.

In 1984, I answered God's call to ministry and founded Whole Life Ministries in Augusta, Georgia. We are a non-denominational church and we teach the full Gospel. When the Lord gave me the vision, He gave me a Scripture, which He said was foundational to the ministry: "*And the very God of peace sanctify you wholly; and I pray God your whole spirit and soul and body be preserved blameless unto the coming of our Lord Jesus Christ*" (1 Thess. 5:23). That verse speaks of wholeness in our entire being—spirit, soul, and body. That is His intent—to bring wholeness to His people in every area of their lives—wholeness in spirit, soul, and body. That's the reason the Lord named our ministry "Whole Life" Ministries. He wants us whole—nothing missing, nothing broken, nothing lacking.

As I said, a part of the vision from the Lord included a healing ministry, and He instructed me to establish healing teams and a healing center. In order to establish a strong foundation for the healing ministry, I took an entire year to teach my congregation the Word of God concerning healing. As I taught, I began to see my church members healed, proving the healing power of God's Word.

Our healing teams have truly impacted our community as they go into private homes, hospitals, and other medical facilities and minister the Word of God. They teach the patient what God's Word says about healing, and then they anoint them with oil and pray. Our healing team members are trained and equipped so that when under pressure from critical or life-threatening situations, the Word immediately begins to flow out of them with its healing, restoring power. We saw this so mightily with a young lady who had been pronounced brain-dead and the physicians were pressuring the family to take her off life support and let her go. Before agreeing to that, the family called and asked for a healing team to come to the hospital and minister to her. On arrival at the intensive care unit, our team encountered a pale young lady on a ventilator with no signs of life. The team began to administer the "medication" of the Word. After a while her eyes opened, and she began to follow the team's movements with her eyes. That's the only thing that changed, but when the team left they knew the power of God's Word was working in her. Four weeks later, that young lady came to see us at the ministry. She wanted to show us what the Word of God had done for her. She had regained all of her mental faculties and ability to speak, though she was not yet able to walk. She came in a wheelchair, but by the time she left she was walking! Glory to God! She is one of several brain-dead people we have seen the Lord heal through our healing team ministry.

I held the vision for a healing center in my heart for years, waiting for the Lord to let me know when it was time. Kenneth E. Hagin, who was one of my spiritual fathers, in one of his conferences pointed to me and said, "God says now is the time. And you know what I'm talking about." I began to make preparations, and we opened The Healing Center in January 2000. We were honored to have Dr. and Mrs. Hagin come dedicate the facility to God and pronounce His blessings upon it.

The Healing Center is attended by people from across the United States and from many nations. Repeatedly, people tell us that when they enter the facility they sense the peace and presence of God. It is a beautiful, Christ-centered facility where God and His Word are exalted. The concept is very simple. We teach people about the power of God's Word to heal them and transform their lives. We teach them how to stand on God's Word and receive healing for themselves.

We work in harmony with the medical community. We encourage participants to continue to see their physicians and take their medications as prescribed. We teach them to pray for their physicians to receive God's wisdom concerning their care, and we always encourage our participants to have their healing confirmed by medical doctors. We teach them to pray over their medications and teach them how to go through chemotherapy and radiation without adverse side effects by believing and confessing God's Word. An excellent example was a lady who was going to receive a powerful combination of chemotherapy drugs. The physician had told her she would become violently ill as soon as the medication began to be administered, and they assigned nurses to care for her during the infusion. She completed the treatment with *no* side effects and left the infusion facility with the doctors and nurses in amazement! After all, the Bible does tell us that if we receive any poisonous thing, it will by no means harm us (see Mark 16:18). She is living proof of the truth and power of that Scripture.

People often ask, "How much does it cost to come to The Healing Center?" One of our greatest joys is to tell them there is no charge. We consider it a gift from the Lord and this ministry.

I have been privileged to minister and pray for thousands of people who needed healing over the years, and I've seen God do marvelous things. I've seen people rise up out of their wheelchairs who previously could not walk. I've seen deaf people begin to hear. I've seen tumors disappear. I remember when I was conducting a healing service in North Carolina, praying for people in the healing line. I prayed for a lady and then moved on to pray for others. In a few minutes I heard that lady calling out colors, "red... yellow...blue...green." I went back over to her to find out what was happening. She was calling out the colors in the flags on the stage. She explained to me that previously she had an "eye transplant," but it had died and become disconnected from the socket. She had no sight in that eye. After I prayed with her, she began to see out of the eye that was previously dead! Her eye had been totally healed and her sight restored! How awesome is our God!

It's so wonderful to see the power of God working in healing services, and I'm so thankful to Him for the many He has touched and transformed over the years. However, I teach the best way for anyone to receive their healing is through the power of God's Word. People aren't always able to get to healing services or find someone to pray for them who is moving in a healing anointing. Obviously, I believe in praying for the sick by anointing with oil and laying on of hands. But my main emphasis is to teach people how to stand on the Word of God and believe for themselves rather than depending on someone else. When you know God's Word and know how to stand on the Word, believing for healing, you can expect to have victory in every situation all the days of your life! Knowing the power that's in God's Word will absolutely transform your life! God has greatly blessed us by allowing us to teach the magnificent healing power of God's Word and see so many set free from sickness and disease and pain. I believe we are simply carrying out the mandate of the Lord: "Go ye into all the world. Preach the gospel and heal the sick!"

Now...on to the rest of the story.

Chapter 2

I GOT MY MIRACLE!

What happened, you ask, to my lip? Well, it was a day that started out like any other day. I had no idea when I got up that morning that the day was going to be quite traumatic. Sometimes life comes at you fast and comes at you hard. It's good to be prepared in your spirit and soul for those times. What makes us be prepared? Knowing the Word of God. I'm constantly filling myself with His Word. For me, it's just second nature to begin to speak God's Word when trouble arises.

So there I was, in my home with my little sheltie named Precious. I had been sitting on my sofa and reading, and she was sitting by me on the floor. I was getting up from the sofa, and as I bent forward she jumped up, our heads hit, and as she came back down her mouth caught my lip. Blood was gushing everywhere. I grabbed a towel, and because of the profuse bleeding I called some friends and said, "I think I need to go to the hospital." The first thing I heard when I got to the emergency room was the nurse asking me, "Where is your lip?" My answer to her was, "I don't know." I hadn't realized my top lip, from my nose to the corner of my mouth, was missing; it had been torn off.

They called in a plastic surgeon and the first thing he said to me was, "This cannot be fixed." He said, "If it had been your bottom lip, it would restore itself. The bottom lip can do that, but the top lip cannot. We can do some things, but there is no way we can restore your lip back to the way it was." He said we needed to go to surgery immediately. Because the tear was ragged, he had to actually cut more of the lip out so it would be a straight cut and heal properly.

This man told me I would never be able to smile again. He told me it would take three to six surgeries for it to be anywhere close to appearing normal. Before he took me to surgery, I grabbed his hands and said, "Before I let you take me in there, I'm going to pray over you! This is my lip, my face, and you're going to let me pray!" And I prayed that God would be in charge of the surgery and that He would work through the surgeon's hands.

At some point, I woke up on the operating table hearing him tell the nurse, "I don't know why...I normally sew the bottom lip and the top lip together and three weeks later come back and slit it open, but for some reason, I feel I'm not to do that." I knew that was the Lord's intervention. When I came out of surgery he told my friends the same thing he had told me: "It will take three to six surgeries for her lip to have any chance of looking halfway normal. She will never smile again." But I looked at him and immediately I said, "Yes, I will! I *will* have a smile again! My God will do that for me! And I will never have to have another surgery!"

I truly believe that if I had not spoken that, I might have been permanently disfigured. I absolutely refused to receive those words he was speaking. We know, according to the Bible, that life and death are in the power of the tongue (see Prov. 18:21). Our words have power to create our circumstances based on what's being spoken. I could not let those words of his be spoken and left to stand. I had to counteract them with a positive confession based on God's Word. I knew my God was bigger than this thing, and He would bring me through.

When I came back to my church office a couple of days later, I looked awful. My face was horrible to look at. The doctor had put black sutures in and around my mouth. It looked like my nose was sitting more on the side of my face than in the middle. When I went back for a follow-up visit, he pulled out a book of pictures of people who had lip surgeries, people who had cleft lips and other deformed features. Those pictures were awful to look at. He was trying to show me what I was going to be dealing with. I absolutely refused to look at those pictures. I told him, "I *will not* look at that book! My God will heal me and you will be amazed!" I wasn't about to look at those pictures and let those images be in my mind and get down into my heart. I went home and found every picture I could find of myself with a beautiful smile and I taped them all over my house—on every mirror, all over my walls, on my kitchen cabinets, everywhere. I would look at those pictures and I would say, "I *will* have a pretty smile again! Lip, you listen to me. Re-shape yourself, in the name of the Lord! I command you in the name of Jesus to move and straighten yourself out!"

I'm not saying it was easy and just a breeze. I can remember the day I walked into the church service for the first time since the accident. The men's choir was singing. When they saw me, the singing came to a halt. They were stunned by my appearance. Many of them were actually crying. I really looked horrible. Every time I looked in the mirror I saw that horrible sight. And of course, the enemy was always whispering and bringing thoughts like, "You'll never be the same. You'll always look horrible." I had to fight those thoughts. I had to reject them and speak the opposite of what the enemy was trying to get me to believe.

Just ten days after my accident, we would be holding a conference at our church, and I was scheduled to conduct a Healing Explosion where I teach on the power of God's Word to bring healing. My staff assumed I would cancel the meeting because I looked so horrible. And besides that, I could barely talk! I still had the black sutures in and around my mouth, my nose was sitting crooked, and I could only talk out of the side of my mouth. But I was determined to go and do that meeting! I can remember it like it was yesterday. My message was based on Mark 11:23, which says, "*Whosoever shall say unto this mountain, Be thou removed, and be thou cast into the sea; and shall not doubt in his heart, but shall believe that those things which he saith shall come to pass; he shall have whatsoever he saith.*" I taught them, "You're a WHOSOEVER going after your WHATSOEVER!" I was helping them to know they were going after their healing by believing and not doubting, and I was determined that I was going after my healing too!

I'm sure it was hard to understand me because I was speaking through one little corner of my mouth. But I taught the Word. And then I looked at the audience and said, "OK...it's every man for himself!" And I turned my back to the audience and began to praise the Lord, and then I threw my hands in the air and I started talking to that lip. I told it to move, to re-shape itself and grow back in the Name of Jesus. And you know what? It began to move! It was just a little movement, a tiny little movement, but I was so encouraged. My lip had moved! And I began to scream and shout. And then the people began to scream and shout with me. And they began to receive miracles too! I looked the same, but I knew something had changed. I continued to speak God's Word day in and day out, and I continued to speak to my lip in the Name of Jesus. And I kept on looking at those pictures of me with a beautiful smile and speaking that I would look like that again. And guess what? Before long, my lip started looking different, started looking better. I had gone back to the doctor a couple of times, and he was astounded and said, "Well, keep on doing whatever it is you're doing." It was a process, but I knew the power of God's Word was working mightily in me. It took eight or nine months, but eventually my lip looked normal again! And I have a beautiful smile just like I used to! Praise God!

And I never had to have another surgery! They said it couldn't be done. They said it was impossible. But *all* things are possible to him who believes! God is *so* faithful! Believe Him! Believe His Word! Believe for your healing! If He did it for me, He'll do it for you! Healing belongs to you! I hope to convince you of that as you read the chapters of this book.

Chapter 3

HEALING: HE'S MADE IT SIMPLE

Yes, that's what I said. He's made it simple. Jesus did all the hard work. What does He require of us? That we believe. That's all. Simply believe. And then act like we believe.

Jesus made atonement for our sins and purchased our forgiveness at Calvary. He laid down His own life so we could receive forgiveness and be in right standing with Father God. What a love! He put Himself on the Cross in our place and took the punishment for our sins so that we could walk free of sin—free of the bondage of sin, free of the punishment for sin, and free of the guilt of sin. Praise God! We can walk free! And we know that if we fall short, if we fall into temptation, if we backslide, we can go before the Lord and repent and He will forgive us. We'll have a new start and it will be as if we never sinned. And He will help us stay on the right path. He's so gracious and so merciful. He made the way for us to be forgiven and live in *His* righteousness. Glory to God!

But did you know that salvation includes healing for our bodies? Before Jesus was crucified, the Romans tied Him to a whipping post and flogged Him. The whip consisted of nine leather straps, each one having pieces of metal or bone tied to the end so that it ripped into the flesh and tore it off the body. It was cruel and torturous, so much so that some people died just from the flogging. Why did Jesus have to go through that awful, horrendous thing? We know that by Jesus being crucified and dying on our behalf we would receive forgiveness for our sins, and that would open the way for relationship with our heavenly Father. So why did He have to go through that horrible flogging? Was it simply because that's the way the Romans always did it? Well, yes, that *is* the way they always did it. When someone was condemned to death by crucifixion, they always had them flogged first. Was it simply that He was at the hands of those merciless, cruel Romans and because that's what they did, that's what happened to Jesus? Listen—nothing that happened in Jesus' life was outside the will of the Father. All things that happened had purpose, including that flogging. Why did He have to go through that? There was only one reason—so that your body could be made well and whole! We find this in Isaiah 53. Verse 5 says, "*By His stripes we are healed*" (NKJV). Some translations say "by His wounds." By the stripes, by the wounds of Jesus, we are healed. That is the truth of the matter.

Now you may have heard some teaching on Isaiah 53 that says "*by His stripes we are healed*" refers to *spiritual* healing. I've heard that a number of times. And I beg to differ. Let me show you truth. There are a number of ways we can know this verse is speaking about healing of the physical body.

The verse says "by His *stripes*" or "by His *wounds*." That's talking about wounds in His *physical* body. Our spiritual healing (forgiveness of sins) came through the pouring out of His blood and through His death. But our physical healing came by the wounds inflicted upon His physical body.

We can let the Scriptures interpret the Scriptures. Let's look at a passage in the New Testament. Matthew 8:16-17 says, "*When evening had come, they brought to Him many who were demon-possessed. And He cast out the spirits with a word, and healed all who were sick, that it might be fulfilled which was spoken by Isaiah the prophet, saying: 'He Himself took our infirmities and bore our sicknesses'*" (NKJV). In this passage, which describes Jesus healing all who were sick, Matthew refers to Isaiah 53:4, which says He bore our griefs (the Hebrew word translated "griefs" means sickness) and carried our sorrows (the Hebrew word translated "sorrows" means pains). He bore our sickness and carried our pains. This passage in Matthew says that Jesus "healed all that were sick." And then it says "*that it might be fulfilled which was spoken by Isaiah the prophet, saying: 'He Himself took our infirmities and bore our sicknesses.*" In other words, it's telling us that Jesus healing the sick fulfilled Isaiah 53. This passage in Matthew points back to Isaiah 53 and shows the context to be that of physical healing. It's crystal clear. Jesus made the provision for the healing of our bodies!

The statement "by His stripes we are healed" found in Isaiah 53 is affirmed in the New Testament again. In First Peter 2:24 Peter, referring to Jesus, says "*Who his own self bare our sins in his own body on the tree, that we, being dead to sins, should live unto righteousness: by whose stripes ye were healed.*" Peter is restating the principle found in Isaiah 53.

Still not convinced? Let's look at the original language of the Scriptures. In Isaiah 53:5, the Hebrew word translated "healed" in "by His stripes we are healed" is the word *rapha*. You may have heard that word before. One of the names of God is Jehovah Rapha, which means "the Lord who heals." You'll find that name in Exodus 15:26 where God said, "*I am the Lord who heals you*" (NKJV). The word *rapha* means "healed, cured, mended, repaired, physician." Now, is there any doubt in your mind that the phrase "by His stripes we are healed" is speaking of *physical* healing?

And now, one last item for all those who still believe that healing in the Bible is only related to healing of the spirit or the soul. Psalms 103:3 tells us that God not only forgives all our iniquities but He heals all our diseases. That word translated "diseases" is a Hebrew word which means "to be sick, to be diseased." God heals all your diseases. End of story. No more time for debating. It's time for shouting! It's time for giving thanks to God for making us whole through His Son Jesus!

I began this chapter by saying, "He's made it simple." Our ability to walk in healing—to see disease and infirmity and pain leave our bodies—has been made simple. Jesus did all the hard work. All we have to do is simply BELIEVE that by His stripes we ARE healed. We simply believe He already bore our sickness and bore our pain in His own body and therefore we don't have to bear it in ours! Because we believe, we speak what we believe. We say, "By His stripes, I am healed!" We speak it in faith. It's that simple. We believe it. And we speak it.

Now that doesn't mean that sickness won't ever come upon us. We've all experienced sickness or pain from time to time. Why? Because we have an enemy. Jesus speaks of our enemy in John 10:10 and tells us that he is a thief who comes to steal and kill and destroy. He brings illness, hoping you don't know that Jesus made the provision for your healing, hoping you don't know that thing has no right to be on you, hoping you don't know the Word of God; and even if you do he's hoping that you will not stand on God's Word. He's hoping you'll just receive the illness and succumb to it. But you're *not* going to receive it! You're *not* going to succumb to it! You're going to say to the Lord, "*Lord, I thank You that by Your stripes I am healed! Lord, I thank You that You already bore this disease in Your own body, and I'm not going to bear it in mine!*" You're going to stand on God's Word and keep on standing until the thing leaves you!

Let's get one more thing straight. God does not bring sickness upon us. The enemy does. God does not punish us with sickness. I don't know whether you have children or not, but if you do I know one thing for certain—you have *no* desire to see some terrible disease come upon them. Even when you get angry or upset or disappointed with them, you have no desire to see them sick or in pain. You would not want illness to come upon them as a punishment or to teach them a lesson! God is a far better, more loving parent than any of us could ever be. Our heavenly Father's love is a perfect love, a pure love, not tainted by sin and the effects of a fallen world. God wants only good things for His children. He thinks good thoughts and only good thoughts toward His people. He has your best interests in His heart at all times. His desire is to see you healthy and whole, not sick! One of the teachers in our healing center had cancer and came near death. She makes this statement to the students on a regular basis: "God did not put cancer on me. God brought me *through* cancer!" She knows it was the work of the Lord that brought her deliverance from that disease. She knows that God is good.

You may have thought to yourself in times past, *Well, I don't know if it's God's will for me to be healed.* Think about it this way: If it were not the Father's will for sick people to be made well, would His Son have been walking around on the earth healing every sick person who came to Him for healing? No, He wouldn't! But He did. The Bible tells us Jesus did *only* what the Father showed Him to do.

Here's something else you might want to think about. Jesus paid a *very high* price for our bodies to be made whole. He suffered terribly so that we could be healed. He did that because He and the Father desire that we be well. If He went through that horrible, torturous thing in order to provide healing for us, why would God then turn around and put sickness upon us? To do so would make a mockery of the pain and suffering His Son endured to provide for our healing.

I never pray, "Lord, if it be thy will, heal this person." The other side of that prayer, the unspoken part, is, "Well, Lord, if it's not Your will for them to be healed, then I guess they'll have to die." There is not one place in the Bible where Jesus prayed for someone and said, "Lord, if it's Your will, heal them." So why would we pray "if it be thy will"? We already know God's will concerning healing. We know His will by reading His Word. He has made it very clear—His will is that we be healed!

I've heard people say, "Well, this runs in my family." Well, I say, "Run it out!" You are not bound by anything that is occurring or has occurred with any of your family members. Spiritually speaking, you are no longer of the family of Adam, no longer of his bloodline. You have been adopted into the family of God and are of the bloodline of Jesus! Glory hallelujah!

Whatever things have occurred in family members and ancestors, they are null and void in your life!

I hear people say, "Well, you know I'm getting older. And you know what they say...when you get older this happens and that happens." I don't care what "they" say. All I care about is what God says! I plan to be healthy *all* the days of my life! Why not? Jesus made the provision for me to walk in wholeness, and the Bible does not say I can only have good health if I'm young!

Now there are those who say, "Yes, Jesus healed. And yes, the apostles healed. But all of that passed away with the last apostle." How absurd! Jesus healed people Himself, and He healed people through the apostles, and He has healed multitudes down through the ages. I have received His healing numerous times. And I have seen thousands healed by Him. His desire for people to be made well has never changed. The Book of Hebrews tells us that Jesus is "the same yesterday, today, and forever." He has not changed, and He never will.

Jesus, through His death and resurrection, provided wholeness for our spirit, soul, and body. Isaiah speaks of this wholeness when he says "*the chastisement of our peace was upon Him*" (Isa. 53:5). In other words, the punishment for us to obtain peace was upon Jesus.

The word translated "peace" is the Hebrew word *shalom*. *Shalom* means wholeness and completeness. It means forgiveness of our sins and the new birth of our spirits. It means health and healing for our bodies and our souls (mind, will, emotions). It carries the connotation of "nothing missing, nothing broken, nothing lacking." It means harmony in our relationship with God and with others. In a nutshell, it is God's provision for everything we'll ever need in this life! Jesus took the punishment for our sins so we could obtain shalom—wholeness! This wholeness comes from our relationship with Jesus—a personal, living, dynamic relationship. He has a heart to bring wholeness and blessings and transformation to all who walk with Him.

Psalms 145:8 tells us the Lord is gracious and "*full of compassion*" and "*of great mercy*." He yearns for us to be well, to walk in the healing and wholeness He has provided for us. Look at these Scriptures about Jesus:

> *But when he saw the multitudes,* ***he was moved with compassion on them****, because they fainted, and were scattered abroad, as sheep having no shepherd* (Matthew 9:36).

> *And Jesus went forth, and saw a great multitude, and* ***was moved with compassion*** *toward them, and he healed their sick* (Matthew 14:14).

> *So **Jesus had compassion on them**, and touched their eyes: and immediately their eyes received sight, and they followed him* (Matthew 20:34).
>
> *And Jesus, **moved with compassion**, put forth his hand, and touched him, and saith unto him, I will; be thou clean* (Mark 1:41).
>
> *And Jesus, when he came out, saw much people, and **was moved with compassion** toward them, because they were as sheep not having a shepherd: and he began to teach them many things* (Mark 6:34).
>
> ***I have compassion on the multitude**, because they have now been with me three days, and have nothing to eat* (Mark 8:2).
>
> *And when the Lord saw her, **he had compassion on her**, and said unto her, Weep not* (Luke 7:13).

We see over and over that Jesus was moved with compassion to help and to heal. That's who He is. He's filled with mercy and compassion for you. He desires to see you well, walking in all the benefits of redemption. He wants good things for you and *only* good things. Believe that, because He loves you and has mercy and compassion toward you, He will see you through every trial, every affliction. He will help you. He will guide you. He will show you the way out. That's the kind of God you serve—a compassionate God who cares deeply for you. It's why He sent His Son into the world to die for you. God, in His mercy and compassion, desires that you be well and whole.

When I was a new Christian it was hard for me to believe that God loved me. I couldn't imagine that God could possibly love me, that He wanted relationship with me, and He wanted me to be with Him for all eternity. But I had to change my thinking. I had to believe I really was a new creation and old things had passed away (see 2 Cor. 5:17). I had to renew my mind through His Word. I had to believe and accept what He did for me. I had to remind myself, *I really am free! My past has been wiped away! I am starting anew! And my God loves me!* The more I said it, the more I believed it. The more I believed it, the more it changed me. It's the same with healing. I have to believe that He's already accomplished my healing. I have to remind myself of what the Word says about the healing He has provided me. I have to speak that I *am* healed. It's a decision to believe Him as Healer, the same way you believed Him as Savior. We don't have to beg God for anything. We only have to believe Him. Once we believe Him, then we can receive from Him.

I hope you're convinced of the goodness of your God and of His desire for you to be well and whole. He loves you so very much. It is His delight for you to be well, free of every sickness and disease and pain. Jesus came into this world so He could set you free from sin *and* sickness, and He delights in your walking in that freedom. Bring delight to His heart by believing His Word and conquering every illness that comes your way!

Chapter 4

AN UNSHAKEABLE FAITH

How can we have a faith that's unshakeable? By knowing God is an unchangeable God, knowing His Word is absolute truth, and knowing God is faithful to His Word. When you know His Word is true, when you know it's pure truth and it's the only truth, your faith will stand no matter what comes your way. No matter what circumstances, no matter what doctor's report, you will not be shaken and you will not be moved. You'll just keep believing and keep standing until you see the victory!

Everything we need and everything we desire comes to us by faith. Faith is the hand that receives the blessings of God. I'm a faith teacher. Anyone who teaches from the Bible is a faith teacher. I teach on faith because faith is how it all works. It's how the Kingdom of God operates. We are justified by faith, we are sanctified by faith, the Holy Spirit comes to us through faith, we have security through faith, righteousness comes to us through faith, we obtain peace through faith, we walk in healing and wholeness through faith, we have victory over the enemy through faith, we overcome the flesh by faith, we overcome the world by faith. Everything from God is received by faith. Success and victory come by faith!

Faith is simply believing God's Word and acting on what we believe. Faith believes His Word above all else. Faith knows that His Word is sufficient. Faith decides to believe God's Word and refuses to be moved off of it. In the midst of trials and adversities, it's so important that we determine to keep our hearts tuned to God's Word and continue to believe Him, no matter what.

In order to see your faith work for you, *act* on what God has said. So many listen to what God said but don't act on it. People quote what He said. They study what He said. They talk about what He said. They pray what He said. But they don't *act* on what

He said. Listen, I can talk about swimming all day long, read books about it, look at videos about it, listen to experts talk about it, but at some point I have to actually get into the water and start to swim! Faith requires action! All the Lord requires of you and me is that we believe Him and then act like we believe Him. It's that simple.

What does it mean to act like we believe Him? How do we do it? We take one of the Scriptures pertaining to healing and read it and meditate on it and talk to Him about it. For instance, we might look at Isaiah 53:5, which says that by the stripes of Jesus we are healed. We read it and meditate on it. We say to ourselves, "His Word tells me that I am healed. By the stripes He took on His body, I am healed. Wow! God says I'm healed! That's what God says about me, and that's what I'm going to say about me! God has provided my healing already! I *am* healed!" We keep saying it continually, expecting to see that disease leave us.

You have to decide what you think about the Word. You have to decide what you are going to do with the Word. In the game of checkers, someone has a move, then someone else has a move. Well guess what? The Lord has already made His move. What was His move? Sending Jesus to pay the price for our sins and obtain for us forgiveness and healing and wholeness.

Now it's *your* move. He wants to see what you're going to do with His Word. Decide you're going to get your healing and then begin to speak God's Word in faith and keep on speaking it. And decide that you will not be moved by what anyone else says. Keep speaking it, even if your symptoms get worse. Don't give up! Don't be moved off your confession! So, maybe you have pain. Begin to say, "Lord, You bore this pain in Your own body, and I am not going to bear it in mine!" Keep speaking it until the pain goes. It *will* go! That's *acting* like you believe God's Word. If you'll get into agreement with what God has said, you *will* see results!

If I believe that Jesus provided healing through the atonement (which He did), I'm going to stand on that belief because God said so! And I will not be moved by what anyone else says, by what my body is saying, or by what the test results say. I'm going to speak His Word and determine that no matter what comes, I will not be moved off of it! It's a matter of taking God at His Word and refusing to turn it loose. Faith is a *firm* conviction. When you hold a firm conviction, you can't be shaken loose from it.

Where does faith come from? According to Romans 10:17, faith comes from hearing the Word of God. Hearing God's Word produces faith. We can't get faith by having someone pray for us to have faith.

Faith comes from hearing the Word of God. As soon as knowledge from the Word gains entrance into your heart, as soon as the light comes on, you'll have faith. The Bible says the entrance of His Word gives light; it gives understanding (see Ps. 119:130). You cannot will to have faith. It comes from the knowledge you gain from the Word. I hope you're reading and studying God's Word regularly and letting that be a priority in your life. I hope you are "hearing" the Word regularly. There's light and revelation and understanding in the Word! And that's how faith comes.

Proverbs 4:20-22 says, "*My son, give attention to my words; incline your ear to my sayings. Do not let them depart from your eyes; keep them in the midst of your heart; for they are life to those who find them, and health to all their flesh*" (NKJV). This passage tells us to *give attention* to God's Words. This is a key principle for developing unshakeable faith. Giving attention means we read and meditate on the Scriptures, we ask the Lord questions, we seek Him for understanding. Notice, it says they (His words) are life to those who "find them." In other words, there is something to be found. It means we must read the Word as if we are seeking after something, searching for treasure. We are looking and expecting to find something the Lord has placed there for us. If you need healing, "find" the word on healing. Look for Scriptures pertaining to healing. They're all through the Bible. (I've included a list of many of them in the back of this book.) This passage tells us when we "find" them, His words are life to us. They bring us an infusion of His life. It also says when we "find" them, His words are health to all our flesh. Wow! Health to ALL our flesh! The Word of God can bring health to all your flesh—every part, every organ, every system! The Hebrew word translated "health" also means "medicine" or "cure." The Word of God is a cure-all! It will cure whatever ails you!

Some years ago, I was talking to the Lord about healing. He said to me, "Name one reason why I will not heal you." I began to name this reason and that reason, things related to the past. He said, "But My blood took care of that." And then I gave Him reasons people have given me over the years about why they think God won't heal them, things that have caused them to feel guilty or unworthy. Every time I named something, He said, "But My blood took care of that." And then I thought of things in the present, things that may be a hindrance in my walk with Him. He said, "Ask Me to forgive you, and My blood will take care of that." Then I would think of something else and begin to say it and I'd hear Him say, "But My blood took care of that." I could not name one thing that He didn't respond with, "But My blood took care of that." It was so freeing to hear the Lord say that to me! What a wonderful, merciful God we serve! Can you think of one reason God would not heal you? Whatever it is, His blood took care of that! There is absolutely no reason why you shouldn't expect God to heal you.

People of unshakeable faith are people who think like God thinks. Get into the Word and learn how He thinks so you can think like Him! That's when the blessings begin to abound, as we walk with Him and determine in our hearts to think like He thinks and act accordingly. When your car has a problem—some gadget is not working properly or the clock needs to be reset—what do you do? You get out the manufacturer's handbook to learn what the manufacturer says about it. And you learn how to fix the problem. God's Word is the Manufacturer's Handbook for mankind! It tells us everything we need to know about how to live and how to walk in victory.

Psalms 16:8 says, *"I have set the Lord always before me: because he is at my right hand, I shall not be moved."* The word translated "moved" means "to be shaken." Because we have set the Lord before us (we've put Him and His Word in front of us, we're staying focused on Him), we will not be moved; we will not be shaken! The Hebrew word translated "set" in this verse has an interesting meaning. It means to set or place, but it also means "to be like, to resemble, to agree with." Like I said, as we walk with God and study His Word, we'll begin to think like God thinks! And once we begin to think like God thinks, no disease, no pain, no demon in hell can overcome us!

People who have unshakeable faith understand the integrity of God and His Word. Are you a person of your word? I hope so. It used to be that in our society if a person gave his word on something, he was bound by it. His word was his bond. That was a commonly understood principle when I was growing up. I don't see that as much anymore. But that's who we should be—people of our word. When we're people of our word, then we're being like God. *God is bound by His Word.* He is bound to make it come to pass, bound to make it happen. He has said, "I am the Lord that heals you." He is bound to perform and bring that word to pass. It's an eternal, everlasting bond. It cannot be broken. He is bound by His Word to love you and care for you. He is bound by His Word to lead and guide you. He is bound by His Word to protect you, provide for you, heal you, deliver you, set you free. But you have a part to play. What is your part? To believe Him and act like you believe Him. That's all. And because you know His Word is true, nothing can move you from it; nothing can shake you. Knowing that God's Word is true and

He is bound by His Word gives me an unshakeable faith for healing!

Come to know this God who has bound Himself to you in love. Come to know Him more and more by spending time in His Word. Read what your wonderful, marvelous God has to say to you. Cherish the words of your Creator. They are more precious than gold. They contain the very life of God Himself. As you read and speak His Word, the life of God is working in you to bring you wholeness and victory! And you'll have a faith that is UNSHAKEABLE!

Chapter 5

BELIEVING GOD IS THE KEY TO LIFE

If you are born again, you were saved because you believed what is written in the Bible; you believed what God has said. It's that simple. When you were born again, your eternal destination was changed in a moment, and you now have a home in Heaven. You were translated out of the kingdom of darkness into the Kingdom of Light. Every sin you had ever committed was forgiven and wiped away. You were made righteous in God's sight. You became a new creation. Your spirit, which had been dead, was completely regenerated—made alive. God's Holy Spirit took up residence in your spirit to be your Teacher and Guide and to form you into the image of Christ. You were made whole—spirit, soul, and body. You became a child of the Most High God. You became a partaker of the life of God and of His divine nature. You became a joint heir with Christ and inherited all that He has. You became royalty. All of that happened in a moment simply because you believed God. Believing God is the key to life. It's the key to everything.

God is a God of life. He IS life. He is the source of life and all things pertaining to life. If we want the life of God working in us and for us (rather than the things of the enemy, the things of death), we must believe what He has said. God's Word is filled with the very life of God. Believing His Word is the key to having His life working mightily in ours.

The Bible tells us that God cannot lie (see Num. 23:19; Heb. 6:18; Tit. 1:2). God is not like people. He tells no lies. He doesn't vacillate or change what He says from one day to the next. When He says something, you can believe it. When He says He'll do something, He does it. When He makes a promise, He keeps it. You can believe God! Everything He has spoken to us in the Bible is the absolute truth. His Word is infallible, inerrant, and unchangeable. You can believe what He has said and you can build your life on it!

Believing God is your first step toward wholeness and healing. It's your first step toward walking in *any* of the blessings provided by God. We cannot rise above our belief about God. If we believe God is a mean, vindictive God, then we won't expect to receive good things from Him. But we have to know that God is a good God and He wants good things for us. That is the truth. We have to know that God is not mad with us. We have to know He cares for us. If we believe He doesn't care about us, then we won't expect Him to intervene in our situations. But He does care. He cares deeply about all that concerns us. If we believe God is too big and too busy to be bothered with the little things of our lives, then we won't expect to see God move on our behalf. I was literally taught that I shouldn't bother God unless I had some major problem. But I found out that God cares about everything in my life—little things, big things, and everything in between. It's all about letting God be God, letting Him be involved in every part of our lives. He loves it when we come to Him with a problem. Why does He love that? Because it shows Him that our trust is in Him and not in ourselves or anyone else. It shows Him that we have learned to be dependent on Him for all things. And that blesses

Him! As we trust Him and depend on Him more and more, then He has the latitude to express Himself in and through our lives. And that equates to power—power to conquer, power to overcome, power to be victorious in every situation.

You can believe in the power of God's Word. I'm reminded of a young lady who attended our healing center. She had been diagnosed with Crohn's disease, which is an inflammation of the intestines and can be very painful and cause damage in other organs. After new x-rays showed a worsening of her condition, her physician scheduled her to see a specialist. She took the x-rays home so she could take them to the specialist. They were lying on her desk, but it bothered her every time she saw them. So, she turned in her Bible to her favorite healing Scripture, then turned the Bible face down on top of the scans (healing Scripture facing the scans) and left it that way. Each time she walked by them she would lay her hands on the file and say, "The Word of God is greater than this bad report!" She continued to speak God's Word in faith. Three weeks later, she went to the specialist. After reviewing the scans he said, "I have no idea what the other doctor is talking about. There is no Crohn's disease." She was healed! Did you get what I just said? The scans no longer showed Crohn's disease. These were not new scans, these were the original scans! The Word of God had actually changed the images on the scans! It had caused them to line up with His Word! Wow! That's the awesome power of God's Word!

But be aware, the key in this scenario was not the action of placing the Bible on the scans. The key was her faith in God's Word, her faith in its ability to change the situation. She had faith in her heart that what God had said was absolutely true. She acted out of a deeply held conviction, and she got miraculous results. And so can you!

Here's a wonderful postscript to the story, just as miraculous as her healing from that disease. She had been told she would never have children because of the damage from Crohn's disease. About two years after this incident, this young lady came to my church for a very special reason—she wanted me to dedicate her new baby girl to the Lord! I was privileged to dedicate the baby they said she could never have! She simply believed what God had said and kept on believing. And God was faithful to His Word.

Abraham was one who believed. When he was first told by the Lord that he would have many descendants, he was seventy-five years old. He and his wife Sarah had not produced a child, and now they were beyond child-bearing years. Having children seemed to them an impossible thing. But our God is the God of the impossible! Even though God's promise was in the face of everything to the contrary, Abraham believed God. The next time God appeared to Abraham, he was ninety-nine years old. Twenty-four years had passed with no sign of the promise coming true. God once again assured him that he would in fact become a father by his wife Sarah. And he did. Abraham and Sarah conceived a son. It was miraculous. Is anything too hard for God? No!

Genesis 21:1 says, "*The Lord visited Sarah as he had said, and the Lord did unto Sarah as he had spoken.*" Verse 2 tells us Sarah conceived and bore a son at the time "*of which God had spoken.*" In this miraculous event, everything had to do with God speaking. Everything hinged upon what God had said. The critical factor was whether Abraham would believe God and keep on believing. The critical factor for you and me is whether we will believe God and keep on believing.

Abraham had to *believe* what God said before he could *become* what God said. He had to believe it when God told him He had made him the father of many nations even though everything in his life contradicted that. Time passed, Abraham continued to get old, the natural processes began to die until it looked like there was no way that promise could ever come true. That's our God. When we find ourselves in situations that look absolutely impossible, even hopeless,

God does something that no one would think possible, something spectacular. His power is unlimited, and there is NOTHING impossible for Him!

Let's think about how this relates to healing. We have to *believe* God before we can *become* healed, before we see our healing manifest. We have to believe that healing was provided through Calvary before we see it manifested. This principle is true of every area of our lives. God has said that we can prosper. But we have to *believe* we can prosper before we can *become* prosperous. We have to believe what God said before we can walk in the blessings of what God said. Once you have *believed* what He said, then you can *become* what He said.

There will be those in your life—friends, family, professionals, even clergy—who will put doubts in your mind about whether you really can take God at His Word. Pay them no attention. That's a trap of the enemy. Don't fall into it. They will be a hindrance to you in your walk with God and your journey to health and wholeness. Religious folks will try to make you think God is limited. Don't buy that lie. Decide you will believe God. Decide you will believe what He has said and you will not believe anyone or anything that contradicts what He has said. Decide that no matter what it looks like, what it feels like, or what you hear about the test results, you will believe the truth and nothing but the truth! There is no disease, no problem that is bigger or more powerful than God and His Word. His Word is creative and can change anything and everything. It can create what's needed and replace what's missing. I'll share a wonderful example of the creative power of God's Word.

One of our healing teams went to see a man who was in a coma. He had open heart surgery and had many complications—bleeding from multiple sites, kidney failure, massive infections, and blood pressure that was dangerously low and could not be stabilized. Our healing teams minister to people even when they are in a coma because we know their spirit is hearing what is being said even when they are not conscious. They administered the medication of the Word to him and told him they believed the power of the Word would raise him up off that sick bed. After we returned to the office, we received a phone call from a family member who told us all the bleeding had stopped! We knew God's Word was working in that situation.

Sometime later, he began attending our healing center. At that time he was on a walker, on oxygen, and receiving dialysis treatments. We were teaching him the Word of God and teaching him how to stand on the Word to receive his healing. He eventually came off the oxygen! Later, his kidneys began to function again and he no longer needed dialysis, praise God! But there was a serious problem. The drugs they had given him to increase his blood pressure had restricted the blood flow to his extremities, particularly his toes. Due to lack of circulation, he had developed gangrene of the toes and the ends of his fingers. That condition worsened and his physician told him he would have to amputate his toes and eventually the tips of his fingers. We were praying that God would intervene so he wouldn't have to have the amputations done. They scheduled him for surgery to have his toes removed. He went to the hospital the next morning for surgery and was surprised because the doctor decided not to do the surgery and sent him home, planning to do it at a later date. That was an answer to our prayer! He continued coming to The Healing Center, standing on God's Word, and believing for his healing. A few days later he was in our healing center receiving an individual teaching session when all of a sudden he began yelling to his wife, "Take off my shoes! Take off my shoes! Something is happening to me!" When they took off his shoes what he saw shocked him and his wife and all of us. He no longer had gangrenous toes but had grown brand new healthy toes! What a mighty God we serve! Over time his fingers were healed too! That's the creative power of God's Word!

There is no physical condition that cannot be changed by the Word of God!

The Bible tells us in Proverbs 23:7 that as a man believes in his heart, so is he. In other words, he is what he believes. He becomes what he believes. You must not receive the diagnosis. You must not accept that condition. If you do, you will not see your healing manifest. Why? Because you believed the lie of the enemy. You believed God's adversary instead of believing God. If you believe things must be the way the doctors say, then they will be. If you believe that when you get old you have to become decrepit, then you will. On the other hand, you can believe what God has said and stand on His Word and see those things change! People may speak things to you that plant doubt in your mind. You can believe what they say if you want to, but remember this—just because a bird flies over your head does not mean you should let it make a nest in your hair! Reject those words and reject those thoughts! The man with the diseased toes believed what God had said and kept on believing. And look at the outcome! Believe God and watch Him do marvelous things in your life!

Jesus said in Mark 11:24 that when we pray we are to believe that we receive, at that very moment. When we believe God for any kind of blessing, we must have an attitude of faith and begin to act as if that blessing is already ours, because it is. We should respond to God as if He has already granted our request. This attitude of trust means leaning upon Him for what we are believing and simply taking it for granted that He has given us our request. When two people get married, they immediately have a new perspective. They begin to see things from the perspective of the other person. It changes how they think and how they behave. This is how it should be when we receive Christ as our Savior and Healer. He expects us to have a new perspective in which we acknowledge Him as our Healer and believe that He has already provided healing for us. We are to believe that we have our healing *now*, even though we don't feel healed or look healed. It's ours now! Healing belongs to us!

Another example of someone who believed and kept on believing is a lady who came to our healing center who was in need of a heart transplant. She sat under the teaching of the Word, her faith arose, and she believed the truth that healing had been provided for her through the work of the Cross. She continued to believe and trust in the power of God's Word. She continued to speak God's Word in faith. After several weeks, her doctor informed her she no longer needed a heart transplant! In fact, she was completely healed and no longer needed any medications! Glory to God!

All of that came about simply because she believed and kept on believing, refusing to believe anything other than God's Word. Don't be moved by what you feel or what you see or what you hear. Be moved only by what you believe. Be moved only by what you know about what God has said. What has God said? He has said that your healing was accomplished at Calvary. He has stated that by the stripes of Jesus, you *are* healed. He has stated that Jesus already bore that disease, already bore those symptoms in His own body, which means you and I don't have to bear it! Believe it! Take Him at His Word! If you'll do that, you'll begin to see marvelous things happen!

Chapter 6

I HAVE BELIEVED, THEREFORE I SPEAK

When we speak God's Word, power is released—the power to transform our circumstances. The apostle Paul said, "*We having the same spirit of faith, according as it is written, I believed, and therefore have I spoken; we also believe, and therefore speak*" (2 Cor. 4:13). We speak what we believe. Jesus said in Mark 11:23 that if a person does not doubt in his heart but believes those things he says will be done, he will have *whatever he says*. We get what we say! When we speak God's Word in faith, knowing that it's true, things happen.

Things change. Disease leaves. Pain goes. Symptoms disappear. It doesn't always happen overnight, but just keep on standing and keep on speaking His Word in faith, knowing that thing is going to leave you!

The Bible says in Job 22:28, "*Thou shalt also decree a thing, and it shall be established unto thee.*" The Word has the power to establish a thing but only if it's spoken. The Lord said through Jeremiah, "*You have seen well, for I am ready to perform My word*" (Jer. 1:12 NKJV). In other words, the Lord is watching and listening for His Word, and when He hears it spoken He performs it. He brings it to pass. So let's give Him something to perform; let's give Him something to work with! Isaiah 55:10 compares the Word to rain, which comes down and waters seed so it will spring up and produce a harvest. The Lord goes on to say in verse 11 that His Word will not return to Him void (without effect)—it will prosper; it will produce. We speak the Word so the Lord can cause it to be productive and bring forth a harvest. You will soon find that speaking and declaring the Word of God over your life and circumstances will bring positive change and great blessings.

According to Luke 8:11, the Word of God is seed. What do we do with seed? We plant it, and then we water it and continue watering it, and after a time we see a harvest. The same is true of God's Word. Your heart is the soil into which the seed of the Word is planted. How do we plant the seed of God's Word? By speaking it. How do we water the seed of the Word we have planted? By continuing to speak it. Keep speaking the Word each day, speaking it throughout the day. Consistency is key! Speaking the Word consistently will allow it to produce the desired results in your life because speaking the Word releases the power contained in the Word. By planting and watering the seed of God's Word for healing, after time we reap a harvest of healing and health.

When Jesus was confronted by satan, His response was to speak God's Word (see Matt. 4:1-11). He said, "It is written," and then quoted what was written in the Word of God. He did it each time He was tempted by the enemy. That's all He did. He simply spoke God's Word. That's how Jesus overcame the enemy. By the Word. Well, if it was important for the Son of God to speak it, then it must be very important for you and me! He is our example. Whatever you may be facing, know God's Word contains the power and authority to overcome it and cause you to be victorious.

It's important for you to speak the Word *out loud* so the power of the Word is released into your life and circumstances. When God created the earth, He did it by speaking. Look at Genesis 1, the Creation chapter, and you will see over and over, "And God said."

It was through His spoken Word that the world was created. The Bible says we are made in God's image. Just as His Word contains power, so do our words. We literally create or change circumstances by what we speak!

The Bible says faith comes by hearing the Word of God (see Rom. 10:17). The more you speak it, the more you're hearing it, and the stronger your faith will become. Hearing the Word of God and hearing it again and again will ignite your faith to believe for healing. I've always said a person believes what they hear themselves speak more than what they hear others speak. I've recommended to people they record their own voice speaking the Scriptures and listen to it often and even play it while they sleep. As they do, the Word will get down into their spirit, helping them to remember it and live by it.

Speaking the Word is not a spouting of memorized verses or mindless repetition. It's speaking the Word *in faith* and *with understanding*. It's truly knowing and believing it in your heart. When we confess the Scriptures, we should not only speak God's Word to Him but combine it with thanksgiving. For example, if you're going to confess Isaiah 53:5, which says "By His stripes we are healed," you might say, "Lord, I thank You that by Your stripes I am healed." That way, you're making it personal, bringing the Lord into your confession, and combining the confession with thanksgiving. If you're going to confess Psalms 103:4, which says, "He redeems your life from destruction," you might say, "Lord, I thank You that You redeem my life from destruction." Speak God's Word with a confidence that it will bring about changes in your life.

One word of caution—watch your words! Choose them carefully because they will either create a pathway of blessing or curses. Proverbs 18:21 says, "*Death and life are in the power of the tongue*." What does that mean? Simply this: you get what you say. Our words have power, power for good or power for harm. If we speak about the condition or the symptoms, we are speaking words of death rather than words of life. We've all heard people from time to time who say things like, "Well, flu season is coming. I'll probably get the flu." And what happens? They get the flu! They got what they spoke. So, don't speak what you feel. Instead, speak what you know. Speak, "By the stripes of Jesus, I am healed!" You can speak yourself into faith. Even if you aren't convinced yet, continue to speak that you are healed, and after a while you will become convinced of it. If you say something long enough, it will eventually drop into your heart, your spirit. Why does that work? Because you are a spirit and your spirit responds to the Word of God. So even if you don't believe it yet, your spirit will grab hold of it. Don't go around saying, "The doctor says I've got three months to live." If you do that, in three months you'll be dead, not because the doctor said it, but because you agreed with what he said. Instead, say what God says. "I'm going to live and not die!" "He has sent His word and healed me!" "I am healed, glory to God, I am healed!" The more you say it the more it will register in your spirit and the more you'll believe it.

We can't be double-minded. We must be completely convinced of the truth of God's Word and then speak His Word *in faith* and refuse to move off of it, no matter what. The Bible asks the question in James 3:11-12, "*Doth a fountain send forth at the same place sweet water and bitter? Can the fig tree...bear olive berries? either a vine, figs?*" The answer, of course, is no they can't. Let *all* your words indicate your agreement with God's Word. Make sure the words you are speaking are words that line up with what God has said. Refuse to speak anything that contradicts His Word.

Words regulate our lives. The life you're living is a product of what you have been speaking. The words you speak create your world. You get what you say! The woman with the issue of blood was healed when she touched the hem of Jesus' garment (see Matt. 9). Was she healed just because she touched the hem of

His garment? Well, that, plus something else. There were many who were touching Him that day who were not healed. But she had *said* to herself, "If I just touch the hem of His garment, I will be healed." She had faith to be healed, but she expressed her faith through her words and actions. She went to where He was and did what she had said. Therefore, she got what she said!

In addition to speaking God's Word to Him, we are also directed by Scripture to speak to the problem. Jesus said in Mark 11:23, "*Whosoever shall say unto this mountain, Be thou removed, and be thou cast into the sea; and shall not doubt in his heart, but shall believe that those things which he saith shall come to pass, he shall have whatsoever he saith.*" Jesus was saying, in essence, "Speak to the mountain and tell it to be removed and it will be." Many of us have a mountain we are facing. The mountain is the problem that appears to us to be so big that we can't get around it or through it or over it. The Bible says we are to remove it. The mountain can be removed by the power of the Word if you'll open your mouth and SPEAK TO IT! Listen, don't tell God about how big the problem is—speak to the problem and tell it how big your God is!

The verse says "WHOSOEVER shall say." Anyone who is born again is a "whosoever." YOU are a "whosoever"! Therefore, you have the right and the authority to speak to the mountain and command it to be removed. We see in this Scripture that this whosoever shall have WHATSOEVER he says. The "whatsoever" is whatever you're believing for. If you're believing for healing, then that's your whatsoever. The mountain is blocking you from getting your whatsoever. You're a whosoever going after your whatsoever! Go after it! Open your mouth. Speak God's Word to your mountain. Your mountain needs to hear your voice. Every time you speak the Word to the mountain you are shaking its foundation. As a whosoever, you can speak to that mountain that's between you and your whatsoever. Your voice, armed with the Word of God, is the big gun, the canon that's going to blast that mountain to kingdom come! Then you can get to your whatsoever!

When we speak God's Word, it shows Him we are in agreement with Him. Perhaps you are familiar with this passage of Scripture: "*Be it unto me according to thy word*" (Luke 1:38). Those words are the words spoken by Mary when she was visited by the angel Gabriel and told she would become pregnant with the Son of God. What an experience for a young teenage girl—to be visited by a supernatural being and then to be given *that* message! When she inquired, "How can this be?" Gabriel explained simply that the Holy Spirit would overshadow her and bring about the conception.

Wow. That's a lot to take in! But Mary believed what Gabriel told her. She knew his words were the words of God Himself. She simply agreed and then said, "Be it unto me according to Your Word." That's what God requires of us—that we know what He has said, we agree with what He has said, and we show Him we are in agreement by speaking it. Simple but powerful! We have believed, and therefore we speak!

Chapter 7

THE POWER OF AGREEMENT

If I believe what God has said and act upon it, then I am in agreement with Him. And there is *power* in agreement! Agreement can work for you or against you. Think about Adam and Eve. Before the temptation by satan, they had been in agreement with God. They walked in obedience to Him and walked in wonderful fellowship with Him. But satan, through deception, was able to cause them to come out of agreement with God. The devil knew if he could get them out of agreement with God and come into agreement with him, the result would be that he would rule the world. That's the power of agreement. It matters who you agree with!

Whatever I am agreeing with can bring me blessings or bring me harm. For instance, if I agree with the Word of God—agree that Jesus has already made the provision for my healing and that by His stripes I was healed—then I can be blessed with healing. But if I agree with the diagnosis, test results, or with the symptoms, then I empower the enemy to work against me because I have come into agreement with him. My agreement with one or the other determines whether life is working in me and for me or death is working in me and against me. Remind yourself—God is always *for* you! And He wants you to walk in abundant life!

Jesus walked in great power. He performed great miracles and signs and wonders. Those miracles were actually done by the Holy Spirit who lived in Him and empowered Him. Jesus was completely yielded to the Holy Spirit, and He was in complete agreement with the Father. There was no discord, no disharmony. He only did what the Father showed Him to do. He only spoke what the Father gave Him to speak. He was in complete agreement with the Father at all times. And He walked in great power. There is power in agreement. Get into agreement with God, and you'll see that power work on your behalf!

Let's consider Abraham again. In Genesis 17:4-5, God said to him, "*As for me, behold, my covenant is with thee, and thou shalt be a father of many nations. Neither shall thy name any more be called Abram, but thy name shall be Abraham; for a father of many nations have I made thee.*" In this passage, God is telling Abraham that He is in covenant with him. The Lord tells him that He is changing his name from Abram to Abraham, which means "father of many." Then God says, "A father of many nations have I made you." Abraham had to make a decision based on what he heard God say to him. He had to decide whether he was going to believe that or not, and then decide what he was going to do with it. What did he do with it? He began calling himself Abraham! In other words, he began referring to himself as "father of many nations." And because he had changed his name, that meant other people were calling him Abraham. Can you imagine what that might have been like for him? There he was, ninety-nine years old, and he was going around telling people to call him by a different name. And that name meant "father of many nations"! Sounds absurd, doesn't it? Everyone knew he and his wife Sarah had no children. And they all knew they were both well beyond child-bearing years. But they had to call him "father of many nations"! Can't you just hear Sarah? *Dear God, what is this old man doing now?*

I've called him Abram for all these years. Now he's telling me I've got to call him by a new name! You know other people must have been saying to themselves, *Senile old man*. But Abraham didn't care. He knew what God had said to him, and he got into agreement with it. He heard God. He believed God. And he acted on what he believed.

So everywhere he went he was hearing, "Hello Abraham." And when he heard that, he was hearing, "Hello, father of many nations!" And every time he introduced himself to someone he was saying, "Hello. I am Abraham," which is the same thing as saying, "Hello. I am father of many nations." And every time he heard his name or spoke his name he was reminded of what God had said about him. He was hearing it over and over. Because He was speaking of himself the way God spoke of him and others were speaking the same thing to him, His faith to receive the promise was being built up and reinforced continually. Abraham had to make the decision whether to agree with God or agree with his present circumstances. He chose to agree with God, and he received the promise.

Abraham could have said, "Well, Lord, OK. If You want to call me by that name, go ahead," and he could have just gone on with life as usual, calling himself what he had always been called. I believe if he had done that, he would never have received the promised son. Why not? Because there would be no agreement between him and God. But fortunately for him, Abraham decided he would be called by that new name. He made up his mind and said, "This is who I am, and this is what you people are going to call me! You are going to call me the name that God calls me!" What God had spoken to him became a reality in his life. He received the promised son. We have to do the same thing. We have to call ourselves what God calls us. He calls us healed! Call yourself healed and don't be moved off of it by what anyone else says. Simply believe God and stand on His Word. What God has spoken will become a reality in your life! That's how faith works. That's the power of agreement!

I imagine Abraham started calling himself by his new name immediately. "I'm Abraham! I'm Abraham! I'm the father of many nations!" You and I know the devil probably started whispering to him, "You aren't the father of anyone, Abram! And you never will be!" But Abraham ignored those thoughts and whispers. You need to be saying to yourself, "I am healed" and then ignore everything else that contradicts it. You'll help yourself if you'll call yourself well, call yourself healed. You may be thinking *How can I call myself healed when I still have symptoms?* Because that's who you are. You would simply be speaking the truth—truth according to how God sees you.

The Bible says God "*calleth those things which be not as though they were*" (Rom. 4:17). He called Abraham a father even though he wasn't yet. That's how God saw him, so that's what He called him. And what God called him came into being. God sees *you* healed and whole. Speak and act according to God's Word. Call those things that be not yet as though they were already! Call yourself "healed" and don't let anyone dissuade you from it! Their thoughts and words are based on what they see or what they've heard; they've seen you sick and they've heard the medical report. You cannot be moved by that! Stick to your guns! Stick to what the Word of God says! Find some people who believe in the power of the Word, people who will get into agreement with you. Try to stay away from those who don't believe it and hang around with those who do! Proverbs 4:22 tells us to keep the Word of God in front of us because it's health to our bodies. Keeping the Word in front of you by meditating on it and speaking it will keep you from considering your body, keep you from focusing on all that is speaking to you through your natural senses.

Abraham had to embrace what God had said and decide that "father of many nations" was who he was. But remember, he had *no evidence* of being the father of many nations, no evidence of being father of anyone! No one believed he could ever be the father of many nations. No one saw him that way except God. But that's all we need—to know what God has said. Abraham heard what God said and he believed it and received it. He took it into his heart. He embraced it even though no one else believed it, even though all evidence was to the contrary. He could have said, "Well, wait a minute, God. I mean, Sarah is ninety and I'm ninety-nine!" In other words, the plumbing wasn't working anymore. This is the way the Bible puts it: "*He considered not his own body now dead, when he was about an hundred years old, neither yet the deadness of Sara's womb*" (Rom. 4:19). He decided to just believe God in spite of everything in the natural realm going against it. No wonder he's called the father of faith! And we know the rest of the story—Sarah miraculously conceived and gave birth to Isaac. God will do what He says He will do! All we have to do is get into agreement with Him.

Abraham agreed with what God had said about him. What has God said about you? He has said that by the stripes of His Son Jesus, you are healed! *Are* healed! Not going to be healed, maybe one day, maybe someday. No, you *are* healed, right now! God made the provision for your healing through Jesus. Decide you will agree with God, no matter what anyone else says!

Romans 4:18, speaking of Abraham, says, "*Who against hope believed in hope, that he might become the father of many nations; according to that which was spoken.*" He received the promise of God, received a son, *because of what God had spoken.* Now what does that mean for you and me? We first have to know what God has said and then get into agreement with it.

Abraham believed "*according to that which was spoken.*" If God had not said it, Abraham could not have attained it. God has spoken much to us about healing. He tells us in Isaiah 53:5 that by the stripes of His Son we *are* healed, and in First Peter 2:24 He tells us that by the stripes of His Son we *were* healed. If you *were* healed, then you *are* healed. Speak that out loud. Say continually, "By His stripes, I am healed!"

The Bible tells us to walk by faith and not by sight (see 2 Cor. 5:7). What does that mean? It means we agree with God and we're not moved by our five senses—what we see, hear, touch, taste, smell. We believe God, and we stay in faith. You cannot allow your body to tell you whether it's healed or not. Don't buy the lie that you are sick and cannot be well. God says you are healed! Get into agreement with Him!

The Bible asks us a question in Amos 3:3: "*Can two walk together, except they be agreed?*" I don't know about you, but I know about me—I want to walk together with God, be in harmony, be in agreement with Him! I don't want to be in agreement with the devil. And I'm not going to! Every time I'm attacked physically, I'm going to take my stand on the Word of Almighty God and I'm going to be victorious!

We *must* let the Word of God rule our lives. Do you know why we get into trouble? Because we believe things God never said. We believe things someone else said. Listen, doctors do not have the final word. God does! We so appreciate doctors and those in the medical profession, but we also know it is God who has the final word about our lives. You have to decide who you're going to believe.

Several years ago, our Director of Healing Ministries began to experience severe abdominal pain with swelling and tenderness. When she went to the doctor, she was told she had a mass so big they couldn't tell where it began and where it ended. They told her, "If this was a certain type of cancer, as opposed to another type, you would already be dead. But we're not sure of anything at this point." Well, that was disheartening. She was told they would have to do more tests. She made up her mind she was not going to get into fear. When she got into her car, she said, "Lord, I've heard what *they* have to say about this. Now I want to hear what *You* have to say." The Lord answered her and said, "Hebrews 4:12." She looked up the verse and found it says that the Word of the Lord is alive and powerful and sharper than any two-edged sword.

What was God saying to her by directing her to that verse? He was saying, "My Word is a sword. And it will cut this thing out!" She read the verse, and then she said, "Lord, You are the Great Physician. A sword in the hands of a physician is called a scalpel. I believe You will take the scalpel of the Word and cut every lifeline, every attachment of this mass, and it will wither and die and leave my body." Six weeks later, when they did the final tests, they could find no evidence of the mass! Glory to God! She was standing on that Scripture and would not be moved off of it. She got into agreement with what God had said to her and had a marvelous outcome!

During the time she was standing on the Word, believing for a complete healing, the symptoms never left her. The pain never left. The swelling never left. On the day she went into the doctor's office and was told the mass was gone, she was still experiencing severe pain as she entered the medical building. But there was no pain when she left! She believes that thing withered and died immediately after she spoke God's Word. The enemy continued to hit her with symptoms, hoping that would cause her to come out of agreement with God. She was determined to continue in agreement with God's Word and would not be moved off of it. And she experienced a miraculous healing!

It is critically important that you not allow symptoms to dissuade you from your belief and your confession. Keep this in mind—a symptom is not a sickness. But you can turn a symptom into a sickness by getting into agreement with it. Refuse to agree with any symptom. Refuse to agree with the enemy. Stay in agreement with God and His Word!

Please understand this—healing is not a promise of God. It's a fact. It's not something that's out yonder somewhere. By His stripes you *were* healed. It's something that has already been accomplished! God has not promised He's going to heal us. He has told us that we are healed already! So many keep thinking it's something that's way out there and someday they're going to get it. No! Healing is now! Healing is today! Just like salvation is today, not tomorrow, or somewhere down the road. When you got saved, you got saved on that very day. It wasn't some thing in the future. It was right then. At that moment, you were saved and transformed into a new creation. It's the same with healing. You have it now!

Healing for your body has already been accomplished. God just needs us to believe it. That's what Abraham did. He simply believed that what God had said was true. Even though his body and Sarah's body were contradicting what God had said, he chose to believe God anyway. It's the same with you and me. Our bodies are telling us we're sick. But we have to choose to believe God rather than what our bodies are telling us. We have to choose to be in agreement with God.

Stand against that lie from the enemy and refuse to believe it has to be the way "they" say. Believe instead that it will be the way God says! It's not about what you feel. It's not about what you see. It's about what you *know!* It's about what you *believe!* When you have symptoms, there is a contradiction happening. Your body is saying one thing but God has said something else. We have to say what God says. The Bible tells us to call those things that be not as those they were. Remind yourself that the God you serve can make dead things come to life! Whether it's an organ or a limb or a whole body system, God can make that dead thing come to life! Agree with Him and then expect to see it happen!

Romans 4:19, speaking of Abraham, says, "*Being not weak in faith, he considered not his own body now dead, when he was about an hundred years old, neither yet the deadness of Sara's womb.*" He was not weak in faith. What does weak faith do? It considers the body. It considers the things in the natural realm.

But strong faith refuses to look upon the things in the natural life. Strong faith looks at God and nothing *but* God. Strong faith gets into agreement with God. So if you're saying something like, "My faith is so weak; I wish I had strong faith," here's what you do—stop considering your body, your symptoms, the doctor's words, the test results. Don't give attention to those things. Instead, give attention to the Word of Almighty God! Verse 20 says, "*He staggered not at the promise of God through unbelief.*" Unbelief is weak. It's weak because it considers the body or the evil report. That verse says "he staggered not." If you are weak in faith, you are going to stagger. The Bible says we *walk* by faith. It doesn't say anything about staggering! We *walk* by faith!

Abraham received the promise. It all began when God began to call Abram by another name—Abraham. There was a time in my life when God began to call me "preacher." I wasn't a preacher, but that's what He began calling me. He told me He was calling me to preach and calling me into full-time ministry. I had so many people telling me, "Women cannot be preachers!" And I had others telling me, "But you won't have much income. You'll probably starve!" I could have listened to those folks. But I chose to believe God instead. I chose to get into agreement with Him. I left a well-paying position to do what

God told me to do. And I've never regretted it. God has taken good care of me. I have been so blessed in so many ways by our faithful God. And, through the years, I've seen my God do miraculous and glorious things for people who decided to simply agree with Him! There is power in agreement!

Chapter 8

RISE ABOVE!

You were born to fly. I'm speaking of spiritual things. You were born to transcend, to rise above. Think about the butterfly. He starts out in life as a caterpillar, a creature that is earth-bound, knowing only of earthly things. Through a phenomenal process, he becomes a butterfly, a beautiful creature that is no longer earth-bound but flies heavenward, no longer held down to earthly things but experiencing the "higher" life. That's amazing! How awesome is our Creator!

The caterpillar being transformed into a butterfly is a wonderful picture of the born-again experience. We were dead in our sins and trespasses, existing on a lower plane, bound to the things of the earth. Then Jesus came into our lives and made us a new creation. That butterfly becomes a completely new creature, one that no longer resembles its old self. Spiritually, we no longer resemble our old selves. We've been made new! Old things have passed away, and all things are made new (see 2 Cor. 5:17). A caterpillar must crawl on the ground. Everything that lies in his path is an obstacle over which he must crawl. Sometimes the obstacles are large and difficult and he crawls over with much effort and exhaustion. But then, metamorphosis happens. He is transformed into a butterfly. And now, all he has to do is fly over those obstacles in his path. It's the same for you and me. We were born anew in Christ, and we were born to rise above!

There will never be anything—no situation, no circumstance—in your life that you cannot rise above! Never! The One who rose from the grave lives in you! Through the Cross, He conquered sin and all that came with it—disease, pain, poverty, depravity, depression. And when He rose from the grave, He conquered death. Everything that comes into your life that causes you frustration—disease, pain, lack—all of it is brought by the enemy who is over the kingdom of death. But praise God, Jesus conquered death and everything associated with it! And because He rose up, *you* can rise up! You no longer have to be held down by the workings of the enemy. When going through adversity, remind yourself the Bible tells us that all things are possible with God and nothing shall be impossible (see Mark 9:23; Matt. 19:26; Luke 1:37; 18:27). Because nothing is impossible with God, you can rise above every situation, every difficulty!

One of the many people touched by Jesus was a blind man named Bartimaeus who came to Him for healing. Mark's account begins with Bartimaeus sitting by the roadside begging for coins. Look at what he did when he heard Jesus was coming his way:

> *And when he heard that it was Jesus of Nazareth, he began to cry out, and say, Jesus, thou Son of David, have mercy on me* (Mark 10:47).

He cried out, "Son of David, have mercy on me!" Why is that significant? Because "Son of David" was a Messianic title, a title reserved for the One who was to come, the Messiah. We can hear his faith in what he was saying. He believed in Jesus. He believed in his heart that Jesus was the Messiah. Let's see what happens next:

> *And many charged him that he should hold his peace: but he cried the more a great deal, Thou Son of David, have mercy on me. And Jesus stood still, and commanded him to be*

> *called. And they called the blind man, saying unto him, Be of good comfort, rise; he calleth thee. And he, casting away his garment, rose, and came to Jesus. And Jesus answered and said unto him, What wilt thou that I should do unto thee? The blind man said unto him, Lord, that I might receive my sight. And Jesus said unto him, Go thy way; thy faith hath made thee whole. And immediately he received his sight, and followed Jesus in the way* (Mark 10:48-52).

How awesome is our Lord! What a magnificent miracle! What I love about Bartimaeus is his strong faith. They told him to hush up and be quiet because, after all, he was just a beggar, a no-account. But he kept on crying out because he knew that Man could help him. He knew that Man could change his whole life. Jesus was walking and moving along with all His followers crowded around Him clamoring for attention, but when He heard that cry, He stopped. He stood still. Jesus always hears our cry and always responds to us. There will never be a time when you cry out to Him that He doesn't hear and respond. Jesus heard Bartimaeus and then commanded that he come to Him. Now watch the faith of this man. Bartimaeus jumped up, casting away his garment as he arose. He cast away his garment! Why is that significant? Because a beggar was required to wear a beggar's garment. That garment was the evidence that he had been examined by the priests and was genuine in his claim to being blind and being eligible to beg for money. But when he heard that Jesus was calling him, he threw that thing off! Think about it. He had not been healed yet. He hadn't even gone to where Jesus was yet. But when he arose, he threw that beggar's garment off! It was as if he were saying, "I'm done with being a beggar! I'm done with being blind! I'm throwing off my old life and my old ways of living! I'm about to start a whole new life!" That's what we need to do. Throw off that disease! Throw off that lifestyle of living with those symptoms and being content to be in that state. Throw if off by the power of God's Word! Let all of Heaven and all of hell know that you've decided you'll no longer live that way!

The passage says, "*They called the blind man, saying unto him, Be of good comfort, rise.*" They told him to rise, and that's just what he did. He rose up physically, but he was also rising up spiritually. He was rising above his situation, rising above his infirmity, rising above all that had been holding him down. And so can you. Rise up! Rise above it! Decide that you will no longer be subject to that infirmity, no longer subject to that pain. You have God's Word on the matter! Rise up!

I heard a story about an old woman who had baked some biscuits and they came out flat. Someone asked her why they were flat. She said, "Well, they squatted to rise, but they got baked in a squat." So, I say to you—DON'T GET BAKED IN A SQUAT! When the heat is on—the heat of a fiery trial—rise up and rise above it!

Your faith in God will bring about God's purposes in your life. God knows the call on your life, and He will test your faith by allowing difficulties from time to time. At times you may feel like those biscuits, like you've been put into a hot oven. But just know you're coming out. His purpose in allowing trials is so you can be promoted to higher ground. His intent is that you move up higher. A perfect example of this principle is found in the story of Joseph, the son of Jacob. Joseph was hit with adversities time and time again and kept rising above them. He was in the midst of fiery trials but was not going to allow himself to be "baked in a squat." He kept on rising, kept on moving higher and higher by the grace of God.

Joseph was born into a wealthy family. He had all that he needed, more than enough. Life was good. And then one day, everything changed. His life was turned upside down. He was betrayed by those who were supposed to love him, his own brothers. They threw him into a pit. It doesn't get lower than a pit.

And it's dark in a pit. Do you sometimes feel like you're in a low place that's dark, like you're in a pit and can't climb out? Has that disease overwhelmed you and caused you to feel you're surrounded with darkness and you can't see the light? Fear not, only believe! God has, through the death and resurrection of Jesus, extended His strong arm down to you and lifted you up out of that pit! Believe in the power of God's Word and the power of the Cross! Your knowing and believing will bring you out of that dark, low place. Your faith in God's Word will bring you up out of that pit of disease and pain!

We don't know how long Joseph was in the pit, but there came a point in time where he started hearing people talking and congregating around the pit. He must have been saying to himself, "Oh, thank God, I'm going to get out of here! This nightmare is finally ending!" But, alas, it was not to be. He was helped out of the pit all right, only to be given into the hands of merchants who were on their way to Egypt. How awful that had to be. He was given over to Ishmaelites, sworn enemies of Israel who probably did not treat him kindly. He was being taken on some journey to someplace, not knowing his destination. Sometimes it can feel like life has taken us on a journey we don't want to be on. If it's a journey of illness and affliction, be of good courage, for you already know your destination. Your destination is healing and wholeness! That's what your Lord has provided for you!

Joseph was taken to Egypt and sold on the slave block. He was sold to Potiphar, an officer of Pharaoh. What a situation he finds himself in. This one who came from a wealthy family, having all he could ever want, had all of his possessions taken away from him, and he himself became property! He was sold into bondage as a slave. But God was with him. He caused Joseph to have favor with Potiphar who put him in charge as overseer in his house. Joseph became the steward over all that Potiphar owned. Because of the favor of God, Joseph rose above his lowly station as a slave and became the trusted steward in the house of an officer of Pharaoh. When you trust in God, He'll cause you to rise above any and every circumstance! Hold on to your faith in Him like Joseph did. Maintain your hope in Him, even when the situation seems grim. Remind yourself there is a light at the end of this tunnel. There is an end to this trial. A good end. An expected end. The Lord says to you, "*I know the thoughts I think toward you...thoughts of peace, and not of evil, to give you an expected end*" (Jer. 29:11).

Things were going great for Joseph until one day Potiphar's wife decided she liked Joseph...liked him a little too much. She tried to tempt him into having an affair with her, but being a man of integrity he flatly refused. His answer to her was, "How can I do such a wicked thing to my master who has been so kind to me and trusts me with all he has? And how could I sin in that way against God?" She continued in her tempting day after day, but Joseph would not relent. Finally, she was so incensed and irate that she brought a charge of assault against him. Although the charge was completely false, Potiphar hearkened to his wife and had Joseph thrown into prison.

Thrown into prison! What a turn of events in his life! He had been a trusted, well-respected steward for an important man in Egypt, and now he finds himself in prison! All his freedom has been completely taken away and he is in captivity. Sometimes we can feel like we're bound and in a prison when we have chronic illness and symptoms that persist. There's this doctor visit and that doctor visit, there's this treatment and that treatment, there's this medication and that medication. And it goes on and on. You may be feeling there is no way out. But I've got good news for you. God tells us in First Corinthians 10:13 that even though trials will come, He will always provide a way of escape. So don't lose heart. Jesus has made the way of escape from disease and pain through the Cross of Calvary! He paid the price so you could be free from every disease!

Well, things were looking pretty bad in Joseph's life at this point. He had been imprisoned even though he was innocent, all his freedom taken away. But God was with him and before long gave him favor with the prison keeper. He put Joseph in charge of the prisoners and all that went on in the prison. He was over all things, second only to the prison keeper. He had gained back a measure of freedom. That's our God. Whenever the enemy subtracts, God always adds back. But He doesn't just add back, He multiplies. He goes above and beyond anything we can ask or imagine. You'll see that when we get to the end of this story. It says in Genesis 39:23 that the prison keeper gave no attention to anything in Joseph's charge because he saw the Lord was with Joseph and made whatever he did to prosper. When we walk with the Lord, walking in His ways, He will make all that we do prosper; in other words, He will make us have good success in every endeavor and through every difficulty. We will be successful in conquering that illness and every other adversity because the Lord is with us and has put His favor upon us.

The story of Joseph's life has a marvelous ending. Because of his gift of dream interpretation, he was brought before Pharaoh and through a series of events was made the number two official over the entire kingdom of Egypt! He had the favor of the king and even lived in the king's palace. Life is funny. Sometimes we have to arrive at our "palace" by way of a "prison." But take heart—we have the King's favor, and His favor is working for us continually. His favor will lift us out of our circumstances, cause us to rise and soar above it!

It's like what the eagle does. The eagle knows when a storm is approaching long before it breaks. Other animals and birds will run and hide from the storm. But not the eagle. He will fly to some high spot and wait for the winds to come. In other words, he confronts the storm; he doesn't hide from it. When the storm hits, he sets his wings so that the wind will pick him up and lift him above the storm. While the storm rages below, the eagle is soaring high above. The eagle does not escape the storm; he simply uses the storm to lift himself higher and rise above it. He rises on the winds that brought the storm! Be like the eagle. Let the storms of life propel you to a higher place. The higher you go in faith, the more you can see from a heavenly perspective. God doesn't just want you healed of that disease, He wants you well and whole and living a vibrant life!

The Bible says to us, "Arise, shine; for your light has come!" (Isa. 60:1). And I say to you, "Arise from that sickbed and shine forth the glory of God in your life—the glory of having overcome, having conquered that disease and those symptoms through the power of God's Word!" Your light has come—the light of the truth of the Gospel of Jesus Christ, the Gospel that tells us He conquered death and sickness and pain. And so can you. You were born to transcend every circumstance! You were born to rise up and rise above!

Chapter 9

KEEP YOUR EYES ON JESUS

In the previous chapter, I talked about rising above circumstances. What helps us rise above and stay above? Keeping our eyes on Jesus. It really is that simple. Let's imagine Jesus saying to us, "If you keep your eyes on Me, you can walk on water!" Peter did it. Why was he able to do such a phenomenal thing? Because he had his eyes on Jesus. Yes, we all know it was short-lived. But he did it. He actually walked on the water! But then he began to sink. That's what the Bible says—he *began* to sink! You don't "begin" to sink. You just go straight to the bottom. How is it that Peter only "began" to sink? Jesus had said to Peter, "Come." When Peter stepped out of the boat, he was literally walking on the Word spoken by Jesus. That's why he only "began" to sink, because he was being upheld by the Word.

What caused him to begin to sink? Because fear and doubt entered in. Peter started looking at the storm, hearing the howling winds, and seeing the height of the waves. And fear and doubt entered into his heart. Why? Because he took his eyes off Jesus. When you're going through a storm—an adversity, some trouble, a terrible report from the doctor—keep your eyes on Jesus and don't take them off Him. I cannot emphasize how critically important this is. No matter what you hear, no matter what you feel, do not take your eyes off Jesus! If you keep your eyes on Him you'll be able to rise above that storm instead of sinking under the weight of it.

When you're looking at Jesus, you're looking at truth, and that keeps you from being deceived by the lies of the enemy. When you're looking at Jesus, you're looking at victory because He IS victory. When you're looking at Jesus, you're looking at health and wholeness. He *is* healing.

When I say "keep your eyes on Jesus," I mean think on the victory He has already won for you. It's *your* victory. Think on the powerful work He accomplished at Calvary. It was at Calvary that satan and all his kingdom were defeated, and that means sickness and disease were defeated. Think on the fact that He rose up from the grave and remind yourself that because He rose up you too will rise up. Keep your eyes on Jesus and think on these things!

See with spiritual eyes. Look at things in the spirit dimension. What are you looking at? Are you looking at the problem, the circumstances? Are you looking at the symptoms, the test results? I hope you're looking at Jesus. Decide that you are not going to focus on the problem. Doing that can hinder your victory. Listen, you can't build a mountain and tear one down at the same time. Jesus tells us to speak to our mountain—the obstacle, the problem—and tell it to go (see Mark 11:23). Jesus tells us to speak *to* our mountain, not *about* it. You'll never see it go if you're constantly looking at it and talking about it. When you do that, you're building that mountain up continually, making it bigger and bigger. How can you expect to tear it down if you are constantly building it up? You can't!

What you look at determines how you think. How you think determines your outcome. The enemy does not want you to put your eyes on Jesus. Do you know where he wants you to put your eyes? On the symptoms, the diagnosis, the prognosis, the test results. As long as you stay focused on those things you are vulnerable to his lies. Don't buy the lie! Keep reminding yourself what God's Word says because God's Word is truth; it's pure truth and it's the *only* truth. Truth trumps the lie every time! Truth triumphs!

It matters how you see. See yourself healed and free of disease. See it right now! See yourself being able to do things you can't do now. If all you see in your life is your illness, you'll never get well because what you look at and focus on will predominate your thoughts. And your thoughts determine your outcome. Look at the Word of God and believe what you see there! Have a knowing in your heart and tell yourself, "These things are going to change. This is only temporary." Rather than looking at the problem, see the solution. Jesus is the solution! Whether it's healing or it's a financial difficulty or a family issue or some other problem, Jesus is the solution!

Grasp the vision. See yourself free of doctor visits, treatments, medications. See yourself free of every trace of disease. Remember Shadrach, Meshach, and Abednego, the three Hebrew boys in Daniel chapter 3? They went into the fiery furnace, and they came out of the fiery furnace. They came out because Jesus went in with them. King Nebuchadnezzar said, "Oh my, I thought we put three men in there. But I see a fourth. And he looks like the Son of God!" He didn't know who that Man was, but we do. He was the pre-incarnate Jesus! He was in the fire with them, and when they came out their clothes were not burned, their hair was not singed, and they didn't even have the smell of smoke on them! No residual effects whatsoever! It's God's intent that when you come out of this disease, this fiery trial, you'll have no residual effects whatsoever. See yourself that way *now!* See yourself well and free of disease, free of pain, *now!* The only thing that burned in that furnace were the ropes that had those young men bound. The thing that has tried to bind you—sickness, infirmity, disease, symptoms—will be gone! You have been set free!

The more you look at a problem, the more you'll believe in the problem. As you look at it and think about it, the problem gets bigger and bigger in your eyes, and eventually it begins to look bigger than God. Remember the Israelites who came out of Egypt? They kept looking at what they saw until what they saw became so big they lost sight of their God. They kept looking at and thinking about what they saw, instead of thinking about who they belonged to. They had an assignment from God. They were to go in and possess the Promised Land. God had said He had given them the land. In other words, they possessed the land even before they went in to battle for it. If you're born again, God has already provided your healing.

It's one of the benefits of redemption. God said, "*My people are destroyed for lack of knowledge*" (Hos. 4:6). Many of God's people don't know healing belongs to them. They live in chronic illness and pain, and some even die from their illness because they do not know healing was provided for them. That is so sad. It's why I wrote this book. I want you to be armed with knowledge. I want you to live long and live strong. I want you to conquer every illness that comes your way, overcome every attack of the enemy. You can do it!

Back to the Israelites. They had an assignment from God. But they didn't complete it because they became fearful. Why? The twelve spies who had been sent to spy out the land came back with a report about what they had found. They found some good things, things that were exactly like what God had said. But ten of the spies focused on the fact that there were giants in the land. They told the others about how big and terrifying those giants were. The people listened to the report about the giants and kept thinking about it and became paralyzed with fear. They became so fearful they said, "We are not able to go in and possess this land!" The ten spies had said, "We were in our own sight as grasshoppers, and so we were in their sight." And they convinced the whole nation to see themselves that way.

It's all about how we see. They saw themselves small, inferior, and without power. What was the result? They did not possess their promised land. Your spiritual promised land includes healing and wholeness. And it's yours to possess because it has already been obtained for you by Jesus. What critical mistake did the Israelites make? They put their eyes on the giants and took them off God. They magnified the giants above God and His Word and His integrity. Ten of the spies came back with a bad report. Two came back with the report of the Lord. Those two were seeing with eyes of faith. But the people believed the bad report more than the Word of God. It's all about our perspective. The Israelites felt like grasshoppers compared to those giants. But they should have reminded themselves that God is a great big powerful God. They should have reminded themselves that to God the giants looked like grasshoppers! They should have reminded themselves of all the fantastic, mighty, phenomenal things God did in Egypt in order to set them free. But they didn't. They just kept focusing on those giants. And they were defeated without even stepping into the battle. When a giant appears in your life, when the doctor's report looms large over you, get your eyes off of it and put them on Jesus. Remind yourself that He is all-mighty and all-powerful and there is nothing too big or too hard for Him.

King Jehoshaphat was a man who believed and trusted in the Word of the Lord. In Second Chronicles 20, we find the nation of Judah facing a dire situation. A great army was amassing against them for the purpose of their destruction. King Jehoshaphat was a man of wisdom. Before he called the troops together, before he made war plans, before he did anything, he went before the Lord to pray and ask for help. He "set himself to seek the Lord," and he called for the nation to fast and pray. When he prayed, he lifted up the name of the Lord proclaiming that He is God in Heaven and He rules over all the kingdoms. He declared that He is a God of power and might so that none is able to withstand Him. Now look at what he says after he tells God about the problem. "Lord, we do not know what to do. *But our eyes are upon You.*" What a marvelous prayer! When you don't know what to do, put your eyes on Jesus. That's what King Jehoshaphat and the nation of Judah did. They put their eyes on their great and powerful God. And God gave them a stupendous victory. It was stunning! Seek the Lord, seek His counsel, keep your eyes on Him. He will bring you through; He will give you the victory!

The apostle Paul had many difficulties in his life. But he knew the secret of being able to deal with the adversities. Let's look at what he said in Second Corinthians 4:18:

> *While we look not at the things which are seen, but at the things which are not seen: for the things which are seen are temporal; but the things which are not seen are eternal.*

We look not at the things that are seen but at the things that are not seen. At first glance, that doesn't even make sense. I'm LOOKING AT what is NOT SEEN! And I'm NOT LOOKING AT what IS SEEN! But it makes perfect sense from God's point of view. He wants us to be looking at spiritual things rather than focusing on things in the natural realm. The things you can actually see are temporal. Look around you right now, and you are looking at temporal things. Everything you see is temporal—people, places, things—they're all temporal. What does that mean? It means they are subject to change, they exist for a limited time. They are not eternal. Now you may be thinking, *Wait a minute. I am eternal.* Your spirit, the person on the inside, is eternal, but your body is not. Anything you see or touch is temporal. We are to look not at the things that are seen but at the things that are not seen. Faith is based on what you know on the inside and what you see with spiritual eyes, not with your natural eyes. We get into trouble when we live by what we see or what we feel, measuring our lives by temporal things.

We've just looked at what Paul said in Second Corinthians 4:18, but now look at what he said in the previous verse:

> *For our light affliction, which is but for a moment, worketh for us a far more exceeding and eternal weight of glory* (2 Corinthians 4:17).

When Paul says "light afflictions" he is referring to those things he mentions at the beginning of the chapter. He speaks of being troubled on every side, perplexed, persecuted, and cast down. In other passages we find that Paul had endured outrageous treatment and very difficult trials. Here are some examples of the difficulties he endured in his efforts to proclaim the good news of the Gospel. He was:

- shipwrecked three different times, one of those times stranded in the sea an entire night and the next day
- expelled from many cities
- attacked by mobs
- imprisoned several times
- hunted down by his own countrymen
- flogged five times

- beaten with rods three times
- stoned and left for dead

And yet, he referred to those things as "light" afflictions! How could he view those things as light afflictions? The answer is in the next verse, the one we just looked at.

> *While we look not at the things which are seen, but at the things which are not seen: for the things which are seen are temporal; but the things which are not seen are eternal* (2 Corinthians 4:18).

In other words, these temporal things, these afflictions, are light when we look not at those things that are seen but at those things that are not seen. When you're looking at eternal things, when you're heavenly minded, when you're looking at Jesus, whatever difficulty comes your way will seem a light affliction. But if you're looking at the problem continually, you'll begin to feel burdened down by it. Why? Because it's becoming "heavy." And the more you look at it, the heavier it will get. Paul tells us when we keep our eyes on eternal things (keep our eyes on Jesus) those things will become "light" in our sight. That's because as we're looking to Him, putting our trust in Him, depending on Him, He's carrying the burden of it.

Then it no longer feels heavy. It's why Paul could call them "light" afflictions. Paul's secret to handling adversities was keeping his eyes on Jesus. He tells us in Colossians 3:2 to set our minds on things above, not on the things of earth. Set your mind on things above! That is a key principle for victory.

What are you looking at? What's directing your life? What's leading you? What is it that moves you, stirs you, drives you? What is it that gives you a reason to live? I hope it's Jesus. Look at those things that are not seen. You can't look at what's not seen unless you have "seen what's not seen." In other words, you've seen Him with your spiritual eyes. That means you have a relationship with the Lord. You know Him. You have faith in Him and you trust Him. Once you come to know Jesus, you come to know that He is wonderful. He's kind, loving, caring, forgiving. He's marvelous! He is constantly saying to you and me, "I am on your side!" And He is saying to us, "You can do it! You can make it! Nothing is impossible to him who believes!"

Let me ask you something. Are you fascinated with God, awestruck by Him? Is He the center of your life? Be fascinated by Him. If your passion for Him has waned, begin to rehearse the goodness of the Lord in your life, remembering the wonderful things God has done for you. Think about God's magnificent plan of redemption and your own salvation. Think about where He has brought you from. Think about the addictions, habits, behaviors, and other things He has freed you from. Think about the healings you have experienced. Think about the miraculous things He has wrought in your life.

Paul says in Hebrews 12:1-2, "*Let us run with patience the race that is set before us, looking unto Jesus.*" In other words, as we go through life, as we run our race, as we do the things we are called to do, we continually keep our eyes on Jesus. Refuse to focus on your problem any longer. Keep your eyes on Jesus and SEE the victory!

Chapter 10

BE COURAGEOUS!

Being courageous is easier than you might think. Why? Because the Courageous One lives in you! The key is to let Him be your courage, let Him be courageous through you. Let your rock-solid belief in God's Word spur you on to courage and a determination to take your stand.

One definition of *courage* is "an attitude of facing and dealing with anything recognized as dangerous, difficult, or painful instead of withdrawing from it." Courageous people face challenges head-on and refuse to be defeated by fear. The greatest example of great courage is Jesus. Think of the challenge that was before

Him—death by crucifixion. That's enough to make anybody run. But He faced it head-on with courage. And His courage lives in you.

Another example of courage is found in the Book of Esther. Esther was a young Jewish girl who lived in Persia. She was chosen by the king to become his queen. Eventually, she needed to request an audience with the king to inform him of a diabolical plot to kill her people. The problem was that if you tried to see the king without being summoned by him you could be put to death. Her uncle Mordecai encouraged her and said, "Who knows? It may be that you've come to the kingdom for such a time as this." Esther went to the king's court and, thankfully, he invited her in. She informed him of the evil plot, the king halted the plan, and her people survived. In this situation, Esther found herself potentially facing death. But she determined to be courageous and took the necessary action. You may be facing death. You may have been given a terminal diagnosis and given no hope. But I want you to know that you have hope! His name is Jesus! Take courage, be bold, take your stand! Speak God's Word in faith, and proclaim boldly that you will not die but live! Victory is already yours. Trust and believe that your future is bright!

Consider the courage of Peter. In Acts 5, Peter and the apostles were teaching the people about Jesus and healing the sick. There was a real commotion in Jerusalem because people were coming from cities and towns all around and being healed. The High Priest and the Sadducees were angry and indignant. They had the apostles arrested and thrown into prison. But an angel of the Lord opened the prison doors and brought them out. He told them to go and stand in the temple and speak to the people "*all the words of this life*" (Acts 5:20). I love that phrase. The Gospel of Jesus Christ is the Gospel of life. God's Word brings life and eradicates death! But let's think about what this angel instructed them to do. They were arrested by the High Priest; he's the religious leader for the whole nation, the top dog. He had them imprisoned for preaching the Gospel. In other words, he was saying, "No more of that!" But the apostles did exactly what the angel told them to do. The very next morning they entered the temple and began to teach the people about Jesus. Those guys had courage! Meanwhile, the High Priest called the council together and sent to have the prisoners brought to them. The prison officers reported the prison door was shut securely but no one was inside! The High Priest was then told that the men who had been imprisoned were now standing in the temple teaching the people about Jesus again! Officers brought the apostles before the council. The High Priest said to them, "Did we not strictly command you not to teach in this Name?" Peter answered, "We ought to obey God rather than men." Truly courageous! The council had them beaten and released but commanded they should not speak in the Name of Jesus any more. I love the last sentence of this chapter. "*And daily in the temple, and in every house, they ceased not to teach and preach Jesus Christ*" (Acts 5:42). They would not be stopped! Because of the courage of Him who lived in them, they were unstoppable! And so are you. The same God who was living in them is living in you. Be courageous! Stand against your opposition—that disease, that diagnosis, those symptoms—and defeat them by the power of God's Word!

If you're going to be victorious and defeat disease in your life, you can't be a wimp. You have to be courageous, willing to take a stand. Be bold like the Syrophoenician woman who came to Jesus seeking healing for her daughter (see Mark 7:25-30). It took courage for that Gentile woman to do that. It seemed at first Jesus was going to deny her request. But she refused to be denied. Because of her boldness and persistence, Jesus granted her request and healed her daughter! Step up, and speak up! Speak the Word of the Lord with boldness! Go after your healing! Refuse to be denied!

Recall the woman with the issue of blood, how she said, "If I can touch the hem of his garment, I will be healed." She was a woman of faith, but she also exhibited courage and boldness. Her bleeding condition made her "unclean" according to Jewish law. In that culture, a person who was unclean had to avoid contact with other people. If they failed to abide by the law, they were stoned to death. What a predicament. She was coming to Jesus to receive her healing. But there was a problem—Jesus was walking with Jairus, who was the ruler of the synagogue. Jairus had the authority to have her stoned for being in public, which, according to Jewish law, was a crime. That would be the same as if you had just committed a crime but you needed to see a particular person who happens to be standing with a police officer. You believe the one with the police officer will show you mercy and protect you from the penalty of the law, but you don't want to attract the attention of the police officer. This woman knew Jairus could have her stoned, but she decided to press on in spite of the consequences. She was "going for it." Her determination resulted in her being rewarded for her faith. And what a reward she received! She was made whole, receiving complete healing and total restoration! What an outstanding example of courage and boldness!

We must be determined to receive our healing and be courageous in taking our stand. Speak God's Word with boldness and confidence. Your Lord will honor

His Word. He'll carry you through and bring you out in victory!

Don't let the enemy intimidate you through the words of others. That's what Goliath the giant tried to do when he stood in front of the Israelite army and said, "Choose a man to fight with me. If he is able to kill me, we will be your servants. But if I prevail and kill him, you will be our servants. I defy the armies of Israel this day!" The Bible says when King Saul and his men heard those words, "*they were dismayed, and greatly afraid*" (see 1 Sam. 17:11). But there was a young man named David, a man full of courage. He was not intimidated by the words of this giant. Instead, he took a stand and said, "IS THERE NOT A CAUSE?" What did he mean? God's cause! He was saying, in essence, "Hey, Israel, have you forgotten who your God is? Shall we not defend the name of our God! Shall we not defend His honor!" David, in the power of God's might, knocked the giant off his feet with a rock and then cut off his head with a sword! Do you not have a cause? Yes you do! Your cause is to be healed because God says that by the stripes of Jesus you *are* healed! Your cause is to be strong and live an abundant life! Face that giant of disease and slay it with the sword of the Word!

The Israelites who came out of Egypt were also intimidated by words. They were destined to go in and possess the Promised Land. But they let the words of others intimidate them and bring fear to their hearts and turn them back from their destiny. The next generation of Israelites would not make the same mistake. Led by Joshua, they would go in and possess the Promised Land. Here's what the Lord spoke to Joshua just before time to go take the land:

> *Be strong and of a good courage: for unto this people shalt thou divide for an inheritance the land, which I sware unto their fathers to give them. Only be thou strong and very courageous, that thou mayest observe to do according to all the law, which Moses my servant commanded thee: turn not from it to the right hand or to the left, that thou mayest prosper whithersoever thou goest* (Joshua 1:6-7).

God was giving Joshua a key. If he kept God's Word in his heart and was a "doer" of the Word, he would prosper wherever he went. It's the same for us. If we'll read and study His Word, keep His Word in our hearts, and determine to live by His Word, we'll prosper, we'll have good success, we'll have victory. The Lord told Joshua (in verse 7) not to turn from His Word to the right hand or the left. What does that mean? Be steady! Be steadfast! Be constant! Don't waiver when difficulties come. Just keep trusting God.

When you keep looking to Him, He will always bring you through to victory!

Look at what God said to Joshua in verse 5: "*No man shall be able to stand before you all the days of your life*" NKJV). Wow. That's quite a statement. That meant that no enemy would ever be able to stand against him. It meant that no enemy would ever be able to defeat him. How is that possible? We find the answer in verse 9: "*Have I not commanded you? Be strong and of good courage; do not be afraid, nor be dismayed, for the Lord your God is with you wherever you go*" (NKJV). That's the key. God was with Joshua. It's the same for us. God lives within you. He has given you His courage and strength. If we'll keep our eyes on the Lord and be ever mindful that He is with us, we'll find the courage to stand on God's Word. We'll find that no enemy will be able to defeat us—no disease, no symptom, no pain, nothing!

One of my church members had to find the courage to stand. She received a devastating diagnosis of stage 4 cancer. She had a growth in her right cheek that eventually became the size of a golf ball, and two small tumors in the left cheek. The doctors told her it was a very aggressive, fast-growing, potentially fatal type of cancer and said she would need extensive surgery that could possibly leave her disfigured. They told her they would have to surgically remove the large growth, all of her teeth, lymph nodes, and salivary glands, and said the surgery could leave her with paralysis of the face and cause her lower lip to droop. They had determined they would not remove the two small tumors in her left cheek, believing radiation treatment would take care of those. They gave her a copy of the biopsy report with details of the cancer, but she refused to read it because she did not want her faith in God and His Word to be affected by it. She chose to believe the report of the Lord that she would live and not die, and she believed God would deliver her from that dreadful disease. Trusting and believing God to bring her through, she consented to the surgery. Contrary to the original plan, the surgeon only removed seven teeth rather than all of them. He removed eighty-seven lymph nodes but only ten were cancerous. She had no paralysis of the face and no drooping lip, praise God! She is certain that outcome was a result of prayer and believing God's Word.

After surgery she began receiving massive doses of radiation along with chemotherapy. Those treatments caused extreme side effects that were almost unbearable. After suffering through nine weeks of daily radiation treatments and seven weeks of chemotherapy, she was thrilled to be finished with those treatments. Unfortunately, scans revealed the two small tumors had not been eradicated. On a Friday, the doctors told her she would need more radiation treatments, which would begin on Tuesday. Over the weekend she and her husband bombarded the gates of Heaven with prayer and continued confessing God's Word. When she went in to begin more radiation treatments on Tuesday, the doctor, for some reason, decided to do one more CT scan. After he saw the results, he came in the room all smiles and told her, "You can go home! There is no cancer! No more radiation! No more chemotherapy! No more surgery!" The doctors call her the miracle patient!

Throughout this ordeal she had been attending our healing center and learning how to take God's Word as medicine and how to stand in faith for her healing. At times her husband would become distraught and concerned he was going to lose her because of the aggressiveness of the cancer and because the extreme doses of radiation and chemotherapy were bordering on being fatal. Whenever her husband expressed fear he might lose her, she would say to him, "Listen here—I will live and not die and declare the works of the Lord! Don't you count me out!" Thank God for her resilience and determination to conquer! She continued to believe God's Word and confess her healing Scriptures throughout the process. She survived an ordeal that for many would have ended in death. I love what she said to us the first day she came to The

Healing Center. She stated emphatically, "I am here to do battle!" She received instruction on how to use the Word of God as a weapon so she could stand, fight, and win. And she did win! She and her husband give all the glory to God, knowing it was He who sustained and healed her. They know with a certainty God is still in the healing business! To God be the glory, great things He has done!

Believe the Word of God. You too will stand, fight, and win!

Chapter 11

KEEP ON KEEPING ON!

OK, you've learned what the Word of God says, you've decided to believe it, and you've summoned the courage to take your stand. Now what? Keep on standing! Keep on believing! Keep on keeping on! It's called perseverance.

God's Word works just like a seed that is planted. You don't plant a tomato seed and then see a full-grown tomato plant the very next day. It takes time. It takes watering. That's true of every kind of plant and every kind of seed. The same is true when you are sowing the seed of the Word. Once you plant a seed in the ground, you keep looking to see if little green sprigs are coming up. Because you've been watering and taking care of the seed, you know it's going to produce. You know you're going to see those little green sprigs.

As a child growing up on a farm, many times I would ride in the truck with my stepfather through the fields and he would show me his corn field. But I couldn't see any corn. I couldn't see anything. But he could. He'd talk on and on about his corn crop, just as if he already had a field full of corn. He knew he had planted corn seed, harvest time would come, and he would have a corn crop. The seed of the Word is planted (released) with your mouth. Then you simply believe the seed of the Word is going to bring a harvest of healing. My stepfather didn't go pull up the seed before the time was right for harvest. He didn't go plow down the little green sprigs because he couldn't see the corn. He waited patiently until his corn crop was ready for harvest. You must believe that before you ever see a manifestation, the power of the seed is working. The seed of the Word is an imperishable, incorruptible seed. It will produce what God has promised it will produce.

Most people want the Word to prove itself first, and then they'll believe it. What they're really saying is, "I'll know I'm healed when my body tells me I'm healed." That doesn't require any faith. It takes a great deal of faith to say you have your healing when all the evidence is to the contrary. It takes faith to say something totally different from what the medical reports and the doctors say. It takes faith to say something different from what your body says or how you feel. But that's exactly what we have to do. We have to believe we have it before we see it. We "see it" first through eyes of faith. Keep your faith in God and His Word and believe you are healed even when your body is screaming at you that you're not healed. Say to the Lord, "Lord, I believe Your Word. I BELIEVE YOUR WORD! And I'm going to keep on believing Your Word, no matter what!"

Everyone loves to receive a miracle, but there is so much value in learning how to stand on God's Word and continue standing until we receive our healing. Once we understand the power of God's Word and the authority we have as believers, we can stand against anything that comes against us and be victorious over and over, all the days of our lives. That's the value of knowing God's Word!

I'll give you a wonderful example of perseverance. We once ministered to a lady who had been diagnosed with bone cancer. The cancer had invaded every bone in her body. At one point she simply moved her leg and her leg broke right before her eyes. At a later time, it was thought she might need to go to the hospital, but the EMTs would not transport her for fear that if they moved her out of the bed many of her bones would break. She was under hospice care, her condition had deteriorated to the point that she only weighed about 85 pounds, she was in pain continually, and she had severe bedsores, some so deep you could see her spinal column. She lived on only a fourth of a can of a liquid supplement per day. Her condition was so fragile her family could not move her to dress her or change her clothing. They simply took T-shirts and slit them down the back and covered her with them.

Because her family hated to see her going through such terrible suffering, every day they would release her and tell her to go on home to be with the Lord. But she refused to give up. She was determined to live and not die. She told us that when her family would leave the room she would turn her face to the wall and say, "Lord, I thank You that I walk by faith and not by sight." She kept saying she walked by faith and not by sight. She made that confession over and over, day after day. One morning, her family came in the room and her bed was empty. They looked around and saw her sitting in a chair on the other side of the room. When they asked, "How did you get over there?" she said, "I walked." She was totally, completely healed! She had persevered in believing and standing on God's Word until one day, there it was—total healing!

Glory to God! After her recovery, she came to visit us at The Healing Center and gave her testimony about how God had totally restored her to health. Our God is awesome! And His Word is powerful!

If you read and speak the Word diligently, speaking it in faith, you can expect to see a change in your circumstances. Don't get discouraged. Don't give up. Be determined to persevere until you see a change. Remind yourself the Lord is faithful to His Word. According to Psalms 138:2, He has magnified His Word even above His Name! You can trust God's unquestionable faithfulness to His Word. Stand on His Word with great expectation!

The definition of the word *persevere* is "to persist in anything undertaken, to continue steadfastly, to maintain a purpose in spite of difficulty, obstacles, or discouragement." Persist and continue steadfastly in believing and speaking God's Word. Keep your purpose always before you, which is complete healing and total restoration. Keep standing and expect victory in spite of what the test results are speaking to you or what your body is speaking to you.

I've talked about speaking to the mountain, that obstacle called disease. God said in Jeremiah 23:29, "*Is not my word like as a fire...and like a hammer that breaketh the rock in pieces?*" A mountain is made of rock. The Word of God is like a hammer that will chip away at the mountain and chip away and keep chipping away until it's gone. Keep speaking, keep chipping away at it. Don't give up.

How long should you stand in faith? How long should you speak God's Word? Until that thing bows, until it yields to the Word of God! Speak and keep speaking until it yields! Continue to speak, "By the stripes of Jesus I am healed!" Continue to speak, "Jesus bore this disease in His own body for me!" Speak the Word and keep on speaking until that disease has left you! No matter how long you've had it, no matter how deteriorated, no matter how bad the pain, no matter what stage, speak to it until it yields! Do not stop speaking the Word, do not change your confession, do not be moved off of it, do not give up, do not give in. Just keep speaking UNTIL IT YIELDS!

The Bible tells us in Ephesians 6 to be strong in the Lord and put on the whole armor of God that we may be able to stand against the wiles of the devil. It tells us in verse 13, "*having done all, to stand.*" When we've done all and are doing all we know to do (believing God's Word and speaking it in faith), we stand and keep on standing. Be firm in your conviction. Be resolute in your confession. Take your stand and refuse to let the enemy or the symptoms or the test results move you off of it. Persevere! Keep on keeping on! You *will* have the victory!

Hebrews 10:23 tells us to HOLD FAST our confession without wavering, and reminds us the Lord is faithful. The Hebrew word translated "hold fast" means "to hold fast, to keep firm possession of." KEEP POSSESSION OF YOUR CONFESSION! Don't let it go! Don't let anyone or anything cause you to lose your confession. Grab hold of the Word of God and keep holding on to it like a bulldog with a bone! That same Hebrew word translated "hold fast" also means "to check a ship's headway, to hold or head the ship." The Word of God will hold the ship of your life steady and keep it heading in the right direction. Sometimes you may feel like you're drowning in your circumstances. Your confession and faith in God's Word will keep you afloat in the midst of the sea of turmoil. This Scripture, in addition to telling us to hold fast to our confession, also reminds us the Lord is faithful. You can always count on Him. You may be in a fierce storm right now, but remember—Jesus is in your boat with you! Keep your faith in Him, keep trusting Him. He *will* bring you through this storm, all the way through, all the way out!

While you're standing, while you're persevering, remember to praise God for your healing. Even when you have pain, even when things look really bad, praise

God anyway! There is power in praise! Praising God in the midst of difficulties is a way of releasing faith for the manifestation of your healing. You might have pain in your body, but if there is a song in your heart and you're praising God, your faith is working and things are going to change! Praising God takes your mind off the problem and puts it on your Savior, your Healer. Praising God and giving Him thanks lifts us above our circumstances. We can praise God in the midst of adversities because we have a confident assurance that He is working and will turn things around. You might think it's hard to praise God in the midst of difficulties, but let me tell you something that makes it easier to praise God—remind yourself that you *already have the victory!* The battle is already won! That's enough to make you want to praise Him! Praise Him and thank Him for your healing even before you see it manifested. When you do that, you're prophesying your own healing! The Bible says God inhabits the praises of His people (see Ps. 22:3). Praising God brings Him on the scene, brings His presence into the situation. Praise can bring forth healing. Praise can turn things around. Praise is a form of spiritual warfare. You may not feel like praising God, but choose to praise Him anyway!

Keep standing, keep speaking, keep praising, keep persevering. In Second Corinthians 4:9, the apostle

Paul tells the Corinthians he is cast down but not destroyed. I like to say it this way: I might be knocked down, but I'm not knocked out! And if I get knocked down, I'M COMING BACK UP! You can bet on that! I know how to persevere. I know how to stand and keep on standing. I know how to keeping on keeping on, no matter what! You can do it too!

Chapter 12

MATTERS OF THE HEART

Proverbs 4:23 says to us, "*Keep your heart with all diligence, for out of it spring the issues of life* (NKJV)." The condition of one's heart is vitally important to receiving healing. The very forces of life are contained in and flow out of the heart. The Bible sometimes refers to the spirit of a man as the heart; at other times it refers to the soul of a man. When referring to matters of the heart, I'm referring to the spirit—the inner man, the real you. God is the Father of spirits. He created us to be ruled and guided by our heart, by our spirit in which He dwells.

God intended for man to be ruled by His spirit, living from the inside out. Our spirit, submitted to God's spirit, was to rule over the soul and the body. However, after the Fall, man was no longer led by His spirit but became a carnal man, dependent on his intellect and his five senses to guide him. Man began living from the outside in.

First Thessalonians 5:23 teaches us we are a three-part being—we *are* a spirit, we have a soul (mind, will, emotions), and we live in a body. When one is born again, the spirit is recreated in the image of God. The Holy Spirit lives within the born-again spirit with resurrection life and power and the ability to quicken (give life) to the mortal body.

When we are born again, everything God has and is, the very fullness of God, is deposited in us. The spirit does not have direct contact with the body. The soul is the "filter" that allows everything God has deposited in the spirit to flow through a man and affect the body and the life of that man. The supernatural flow of life from the born-again spirit to the body can be blocked when the soul comes into agreement with the body instead of with the spirit. The power of God within the born-again spirit will only flow through a clean filter. The filter can become clogged when the soul is flooded with sensory input based on the words and ways of the world. It is our responsibility to cleanse the filter and keep it clean. To do so, you must renew your mind. How do you do that? Simple—you read and meditate on the Word of God until the Word controls your thoughts and decisions more than anything else, including information gathered through your intellect, your five senses, or even what your body is saying to you.

The body is unredeemed. In actuality, it has control over nothing. Most people think the body is the real person—that it dictates whether we are sick or well, whether we live or die. But the truth according to God's Word is that the spirit man is the "real you" and the spirit and soul (renewed mind) should be in control of the body.

It's so easy to live by our senses rather than being led by our spirits (our hearts). God formed our physical bodies and equipped us with our five senses—sight, hearing, touch, taste, smell. Through those senses we gain information and relate to the physical world. God intended for us to use our natural senses to help us live and function in this natural world. However, He never intended that we be guided by them exclusively. We can view life in a totally different way than the world does. We can view life according to truth. The key is learning to believe and trust God. It's a change in mind-set from that of "seeing is believing" to that of "believing is seeing." We can live from the inside out—live by the Spirit and the Word. It's a matter of the heart.

The body is not our real problem. Recall that the Word says as a man thinketh, so is he (see Prov. 23:7). The real problem is our mind. Romans 12:2 says, "*And do not be conformed to this world, but be transformed by the renewing of your mind, that you may prove what is that good and acceptable and perfect will of God*" (NKJV). So the solution is to renew our minds with the Word of God. Once we do that, the born-again spirit and the soul (the renewed mind) can work together and rule over the body. After all, two against one wins!

Jesus had a physical body with five senses just like ours, but He wasn't ruled by His senses. Jesus was the first Man who was spirit-led and showed us how God intended man to live. He chose to submit to the voice of the Spirit on the inside and to the Word of God. He never allowed Himself to be governed only by His senses. We are to do the same. We have to decide to believe and act on God's Word in spite of what our body or senses tell us. Your body may tell you you're sick, even showing signs and symptoms of illness. But the real you, your spirit man, is not sick. The key is to renew your mind with the Word of God, which tells you that by the stripes of Jesus you *are* healed! When your mind is renewed with the Word, it lines up with your spirit, and healing will begin to manifest. Smith

Wigglesworth, the great Apostle of Faith (as he was called), said, "I am not moved by what I see, I am not moved by what I feel, I am only moved by what I believe. I don't ask my body how it feels. I *tell* my body how it feels."

Make up your mind once and for all to believe that God has already provided for your healing and that you are not going to continue to suffer any longer! You can and must take authority over your body and tell it to obey God's Word!

Another "heart matter" we need to consider is "heart knowledge" versus "head knowledge." It's critically important that we believe and know the truth of God's Word in our hearts, not just in our heads. When we only have head knowledge of God's Word, that's called "mental assent." This is one of the most dangerous and deceptive things I see in the Church. Mental assent sees the truth of God's Word, admires the truth, and even says, "Yes, I believe it is truth," but never acts on the truth. Someone in mental assent only agrees with the Word in their mind but not in their heart. It's all talk and no walk. They say, "I know the Bible says God sent His Word and healed us. I know the Scriptures say that by the stripes of Jesus we are healed. I know what the Word says, but...." Mental assent always adds a "but." Someone in mental assent may say, "But it just doesn't work for me." Or, they may say, "I know God can, but I don't know if He will." On the other hand, heart knowledge says, "God can and He will!" Mental assent will not produce healing in your body, nor will it cause the blessings of God to manifest in your life. True faith in God's Word will always produce results. When heart knowledge supersedes head knowledge, you will begin to take action. You will begin to declare, "By the stripes of Jesus I am healed!" You will begin to act like you're healed and speak like you're healed, and before long you *will* be healed! A true receiving of the Word into your heart will affect your conduct, your speech, your thoughts, your whole life. It truly is a matter of the heart.

Now to one of the most important matters of the heart—our walk with the Lord. God desires relationship with His people and He wants us to know Him, really know Him. It's not knowing *about* God but truly knowing Him in your heart. Biblical history is a record of God's pursuit of man. But God also desires for *us* to pursue *Him*. Scripture tells us in Hebrews 11:6 that God rewards those who diligently seek Him. Simply put, He wants us to seek and serve Him with all our hearts, and He will reward us for such devotion. Of course, the greatest reward is to be in relationship with our wonderful heavenly Father and come to know His heart. He desires that we spend time with Him, seek Him, acknowledge Him, learn from Him, and allow Him to be Lord of our lives. It is amazing to me that we are allowed the privilege of knowing the Creator of the universe!

God called David "a man after His own heart" (1 Sam. 13:14). Look at the character of David and you'll see why. David was a worshiper. He communed heart to heart with his Lord. He loved to exalt the Lord, extol His virtues, and sing His praises. David had a thankful heart. In good times and bad, he would praise and give thanks to the Lord. He loved and treasured the Word of God. David was not perfect, but he understood he could repent and ask the Lord's forgiveness whenever he stumbled. David was a man of faith and courage, but his courage came from his reliance upon the Lord. As a young shepherd boy, he fearlessly slew a giant. But before going into battle, he declared, "The Lord will deliver me from the hand of this Philistine." He relied not upon himself but upon his God. David did mighty exploits and accomplished great things for Israel and for God's Kingdom. What was his secret? It was his relationship with the Lord, his pursuing after the heart of God. If we seek the Lord, turn our hearts toward Him, and are wholeheartedly devoted to Him, we too can be called a "man after God's own heart."

You must know that He is an all-sufficient, all-powerful God. He is Lord. He is Savior. He is Deliverer. He is Provider. He is Protector. And He is Christ the Healer. Surrender your life to Him. Let Him reign supreme in your heart. When we surrender to Him, then all He has and all that He is becomes ours. The Lord desires an intimate, day-by-day relationship with you. He loves you so very much with a love that is indescribable, a love so deep and so vast, it's incomprehensible. One of the best ways you can show Him you love Him is by giving Him your time and attention, allowing Him to be your main focus in life. It's a matter of the heart.

Seek the Healer. Fall in love with Jesus so that you're no longer seeking healing but seeking Him. Healing will come. You can rest in the knowledge of His love for you. You can rest in the integrity of His Word. You can rest in Him, knowing He gave His life for you and has already made the provision for your healing, health, and wholeness.

I pray you will take to heart the principles of this book and apply them to your life. If you'll believe God's Word and act on it, allowing it to change your heart and your thinking, your life will be transformed. As you trust in the integrity of God's Word and rest in the knowledge of His love for you, you'll find you have a faith for healing that is unshakeable. You'll be able to conquer every illness that ever comes your way, and you'll find you have the ability to be triumphant in every situation. Just remember—God loves you, and He wants you well!

SUMMARY OF HEALING PRINCIPLES

THINGS TO KNOW

- The provision for your healing was made by Jesus at Calvary. He provided for your healing just as He provided for forgiveness of your sins.
- God's will for you is wholeness in every area of your life—spirit, soul, and body. It *is* God's will for you to be healed!
- God is a good God and wants good things for you!
- God's Word is absolute truth.

- Because God cannot lie, you can believe what He has said in His word.
- God is bound by His Word and is faithful to it; therefore, you can expect His Word to come to pass in your life!
- The Kingdom of God operates in your life by faith—believing God's Word and acting on what you believe.
- You are never alone in your trials. God is always with you and will always bring you through.
- The Courageous One lives in you and gives you His own courage and strength.
- There will never be a situation in your life that you cannot rise up and conquer by the power of God's Word.
- Jesus, who is in you, has empowered you to be unshakeable and unstoppable!

THINGS TO DO

- Renew your mind by reading and studying the Word of God so you'll know truth and you'll think like God thinks.
- Read and give attention to the Word regularly so you'll be prepared when trials come.

- Agree in your heart with what God has said about healing; He has said, "You are healed!"
- Speak the Word of God in faith and speak it consistently.
- Refuse to speak anything that contradicts God's Word.
- Refuse to accept a bad report. Contradict the bad report with the Word of God.
- Stand on God's Word pertaining to healing and refuse to be moved off of it.
- Keep your eyes off the problem; instead, keep your eyes on Jesus.
- See yourself healed and whole, right now!
- Refuse to allow symptoms or the words of others to cause you to fear or be in doubt. Instead, remind yourself about what God has said.
- Walk by faith, not by sight! Don't allow yourself to be moved by what you hear or what you feel or what your body is "saying."
- Don't depend on your body to tell you whether you're healed or not. Go by what you *know*, not by what you feel.
- Expect to see a change in your circumstances.

- Persevere and continue steadfastly in believing and speaking God's Word until you see things change. Refuse to give in or give up.
- Hold fast to your confession. Do not change it, do not be moved off of it, no matter what!
- Praise God and thank Him for your healing even before you see the healing manifest. You can praise Him because you already have the victory!
- Seek the Healer. Fall in love with Jesus!

HEALING SCRIPTURES

God has instructed us to take His Word as medicine. When we steadfastly believe the Word and act on it, nothing can stop the power of the Word from working mightily on our behalf. Let the Lord lead you in choosing which healing Scriptures to stand on. Meditate on them, speak them in faith, and expect your healing to manifest!

For I am the Lord that healeth thee (Exodus 15:26).

And I will take sickness away from the midst of thee (Exodus 23:25).

O Lord my God, I cried out to You, and You healed me (Psalms 30:2 NKJV).

Who healeth all thy diseases; who redeemeth thy life from destruction (Psalms 103:3-4).

He sent his word, and healed them, and delivered them from their destructions (Psalms 107:20).

I shall not die, but live, and declare the works of the Lord (Psalms 118:17).

My son, attend to my words; incline thine ear unto my sayings. Let them not depart from thine eyes; keep them in the midst of thine heart. For they are life unto those that find them, and health to all their flesh (Proverbs 4:20-22).

Surely he hath borne our griefs, and carried our sorrows: yet we did esteem him stricken, smitten of God, and afflicted. But he was wounded for our transgressions, he was bruised for our iniquities: the chastisement of our peace was upon him; and with his stripes we are healed (Isaiah 53:4-5).

Then your light shall break forth like the morning, your healing shall spring forth speedily, and your righteousness shall go before you (Isaiah 58:8 NKJV).

For I will restore health unto thee, and I will heal thee of thy wounds, saith the Lord (Jeremiah 30:17).

I will heal them and reveal to them the abundance of peace and truth (Jeremiah 33:6 NKJV).

But unto you that fear my name shall the Sun of Righteousness arise with healing in his wings (Malachi 4:2).

And Jesus saith unto him, I will come and heal him. The centurion answered and said, Lord...speak the word only, and my servant shall be healed (Matthew 8:7-8).

And Jesus said unto the centurion, Go thy way; and as thou hast believed, so be it done unto thee. And his servant was healed in the selfsame hour (Matthew 8:13).

When the even was come, they brought unto him many that were possessed with devils: and he cast out the spirits with his word, and healed all that were sick: that it might be fulfilled which was spoken by Esaias the prophet, saying, Himself took our infirmities, and bare our sicknesses (Matthew 8:16-17).

And he said unto her, Daughter, thy faith hath made thee whole; go in peace, and be whole of thy plague (Mark 5:34).

And Jesus answering saith unto them, Have faith in God. For verily I say unto you, That whosoever shall say unto this mountain [disease/problem], Be thou removed, and be thou cast into the sea; and shall not doubt in his heart, but shall believe that those things which he saith shall come to pass; he shall have whatsoever he saith. Therefore I say unto you, What things soever ye desire, when ye pray, believe that ye receive them, and ye shall have them (Mark 11:22-24).

Christ hath redeemed us from the curse of the law, being made a curse for us. [Pray: "I thank You, Lord, that You have redeemed me from (name of disease).] (Galatians 3:13-14)

For it is God who works in you both to will and to do for His good pleasure (Philippians 2:13).

Now faith is the substance of things hoped for, the evidence of things not seen (Hebrews 11:1).

Jesus Christ the same yesterday, and to day, and for ever (Hebrews 13:8).

Is any sick among you? let him call for the elders of the church; and let them pray over him, anointing him with oil in the name of the Lord: and the prayer of faith shall save the sick, and the Lord shall raise him up; and if he have committed sins, they shall be forgiven him (James 5:14-15).

Who his own self bare our sins in his own body on the tree, that we, being dead to sins, should live unto righteousness: by whose stripes ye were healed (1 Peter 2:24).

Beloved, I pray that you may prosper in all things and be in health, just as your soul prospers (3 John 2).

ARE YOU BORN AGAIN?

Jesus answered and said unto him,
Verily, verily, I say unto thee,
Except a man be born again, he
cannot see the kingdom of God.
—John 3:3

Being born again is *the most* important event in the life of any human. In that moment, our eternal destination is changed and we now have a home in Heaven with God. At the same time, God comes to live within us by His Spirit. Being born again allows us to know God and be in relationship with Him. He guides us, helps us, counsels us, provides for us, protects us. He gives us His love, His joy, His peace, and so much more.

God loves you more than you know, and He so desires to be in relationship with you. We are born again and enter into this relationship by accepting His Son Jesus as our Lord and Savior. Jesus died on the Cross of Calvary for us and was resurrected from the grave. He allowed Himself to be sacrificed in our place so our sins could be forgiven and we could begin life anew. If you would like to enter into a relationship with God—a relationship like no other—pray this prayer to Him out loud:

> *Heavenly Father, I ask You to forgive me of all my sins. I believe You sent Your Son Jesus to pay the penalty for those sins. I believe He died for me and rose from the grave. I ask to receive Jesus as my Savior. I want Him to come into my heart and be Lord of my life. Thank You, Jesus, for giving Your life for me. Thank You for coming to live in my heart. Thank You for giving me new life.*

Romans chapter 10 tells us that if we confess with our mouth the Lord Jesus and believe in our heart that God raised Him from the dead, we shall be saved. If you just prayed that prayer from your heart, you are now born again, born from above, born of the Spirit! The Bible tells us in Second Corinthians 5:17 that if anyone is in Christ, he is a new creation and old things have passed away and all things have become new. All your sins have been wiped away and you are beginning your life anew!

Welcome to the Family of God!

Now that you are born again, it's important that you find a church that believes and teaches the Word of God so you can become grounded in the Word and have fellowship with other believers. Ask the Lord to lead you to the church He wants you to attend. Begin to read the Bible each day. That's how we grow spiritually. His Word is His way of helping you know Him and know His ways. The Holy Spirit who is living within you is your Teacher and will help you understand God's Word and bring you revelation about Jesus. As you read the Word, your mind is being renewed day by day and God is helping you to think like He thinks. That's how we walk in victory! Walking in relationship with God is a wonderful adventure. Getting to know the Lord is a fun and exciting lifelong journey that will bring you such joy.

Always remember God loves you and you are very precious to Him. He will always be with you and will never leave you. He has a wonderful plan for your life, a plan that will unfold itself as you walk with Him day by day. Love Him. Worship Him. Live for Him. He loves you so!

For God so loved the world, that he gave his only begotten Son, that whosoever believeth in him should not perish, but have everlasting life.
—John 3:16

ABOUT DR. SANDRA KENNEDY

DR. SANDRA KENNEDY is Founder and Senior Pastor of Whole Life Ministries in Augusta, Georgia. She is a graduate of Southwestern Baptist Theological Seminary in Dallas, Texas and is a teacher, conference speaker, and author who has a national and international television ministry. She established a Healing Team ministry which trains believers to administer the power of God's Word to the sick. She founded The Healing Center where the Word of God is exalted, the healing power of God is manifested, and the love and compassion of Christ is demonstrated. People come from across the nation and around the world to be taught how to receive their healing by the power of the Word. Dr. Kennedy conducts "Healing Explosions" where mighty moves of God occur and people are healed. She has been faithful to follow the mandate given to her by God to "grow up the Body of Christ and teach them victory." Her heart's cry is to see the Church become the true Church in all of its authority, splendor, and glory.